THE TOP

100

PROMISES

of the Bible

TINA KRAUSE & MARJORIE VAWTER

BARBOUR BOOKS
An Imprint of Barbour Publishing, Inc.

Member of the
Evangelical Christian
Publishers Association

Contents

Introduction

Have you ever made a promise and failed to deliver? Were you ever the recipient of a broken promise? If so, you join the throngs of individuals who have been genuinely and profoundly affected by a broken promise. Broken promises sting, frustrate, and disappoint. Yet they are a fact of life.

The hallmark of people with integrity is that they consciously work hard to fulfill their promises. When they say they will do something, they strive to follow through. Yet even individuals with the best intentions sometimes fail to honor their pledges.

God, on the other hand, is perfect, faithful, and true. God is not a man, so it is impossible for Him to lie. He doesn't change His mind on a whim, nor does He speak and fail to act (Numbers 23:19). Unlike humankind, God keeps every promise He has ever made (Joshua 21:45; 23:14). His promises and providences are mercy and truth; they are, like Himself, honest and upright. All that God is and does comes from love, and His love covenant with us is unfailing and ironclad. Since it is impossible for God to lie, we can—with all confidence—trust Him to fulfill His promises in our lives.

Although not exhaustive by any means, this book, *The Top 100 Promises of the Bible*, highlights and expounds on one hundred of the top promises of God's Holy Word. As you read, you will discover directives that guide you into Spirit-filled living. His promises will bring you comfort, instruction, correction, encouragement, direction, hope, and insight.

Are you searching for answers to your life? Do you need comfort and assurance? Is your heart heavy and your mind overwhelmed? Are you in search of direction or guidance? Then read on. Allow God to minister to you right where you are. Receive and stand on God's promises. Remember, what He promised, He will do. "The One who called you is completely dependable. If he said it, he'll do it!" (1 Thessalonians 5:24 MSG). That's His promise to you.

Promise after Promise
by Cameron Pollock

You gave Your Word, O God who cannot lie.
Page after page the prophets testify.
And through Your Word You proved every promise true,
Through Jesus Christ, who faithfully followed You.

When Jesus died His dear disciples fled.
How could He fight and crush the serpent's head?
But death would die, defeated within a tomb—
Jesus arose and sealed the serpent's doom!

Oh doubting soul, why do you turn away?
Why still deny that resurrection day?
Come touch His hands; come feel His wounded side.
See and believe in Jesus crucified!

Increase our faith in Your almighty hand.
Help us to trust when we can't understand.
And on that day like Jesus we will arise—
Each promise kept by God before our eyes.

Chorus:
Promise after promise from the Father's hand,
Every word fulfilled at Your command.
Anchor of assurance for the doubting soul,
Every promise under Your control.
Every promise under Your control.

© 2016 by Cameron Pollock; lyrics used by permission.

1. Fear Not, He Overcame

"These things I have spoken to you, so that in Me you
may have peace. In the world you have tribulation,
but take courage; I have overcome the world."
JOHN 16:33 NASB

We live in troubled times. Many baby boomers grew up in neighborhoods where it was safe to play outdoors all day and into the evening—until it got dark—without an adult keeping watch for predators, mostly of the human kind. But our children and grandchildren are growing up in a completely different world, it seems.

News programs are filled with reports of children who are lured into a stranger's car. Many are never seen alive again, and unfortunately many are sold into the sex trafficking world. Even our public bathrooms are no longer safe. Churches and schools now must have security in place whenever they are open for services or classes. Even then, shooters with a grudge gain entrance under false pretenses and at the slightest provocation pull out their semiautomatic guns and start shooting.

We long for peace and better days, more security. We long to return to the "good old days" when seemingly there were no worries, no fear. We long for a better world.

But a look at history shows that none of this anxiety over a troubled world is new. Jesus described the times surrounding His second coming as being like the days of Noah: "In those days, the people enjoyed banquets and parties and weddings right up to the time Noah entered his boat and the flood came" (Luke 17:27 NLT). Or like the days of Lot: "People went about their daily business—eating and drinking, buying and selling, farming and building—until the morning Lot left Sodom" (17:28–29).

In this world there will be hard times, tribulations. Jesus also warned His disciples that all who follow Him can expect persecution for their faith. That was true in His day. . .and it is true today. This doesn't look like the most hopeful of God's promises in scripture.

Until we read the rest of it: He sends His Spirit to each of His followers to restore peace and give courage. Because He overcame the world and death and rose from His grave and lives again, His peace—the kind that surpasses all understanding—will keep us calm and give us courage and faith to face a difficult, out-of-control world. And one day we will live in a new world—one that knows only peace and God's eternal presence.

2. Strong Faith Produces Pure Gold

These trials will show that your faith is genuine.
It is being tested as fire tests and purifies gold—
though your faith is far more precious than mere gold.
So when your faith remains strong through many trials,
it will bring you much praise and glory and honor
on the day when Jesus Christ is revealed to the whole world.

1 PETER 1:7 NLT

In May 1978, a pastor and his young family in South Carolina experienced a severe house fire accidentally started by his two-year-old daughter when her mother's back was turned. Both the mother and young daughter were severely burned and suffered with the aftereffects of smoke inhalation. After months in the hospital and multiple surgeries and skin grafts, they finally returned to a newly built home on the ashes of the old one. But life as they had known it was forever altered. The daughter was now severely disabled and wheelchair bound. The mother's strength was now limited. But through the entire ordeal and to this day, the family has claimed 1 Peter 1:7 as their family's ministry verse.

And what a ministry they have had! God used the fire to uniquely equip them to help many who have been through various types of fiery trials. One of the ministries they established that came out of these tragic circumstances is a Christian school for handicapped children. Their story has strengthened the faith of many over the years.

In the same way, the writer of Hebrews sought to encourage the Hebrew Christians by recording the faith of many biblical saints in Hebrews 11. By faith they "overthrew kingdoms, . . .shut the mouths of lions, quenched the flames of fire, and escaped death by the edge of the sword. . . . Others were tortured, refusing to turn from God in order to be set free. . . . For God had something better in mind" (vv. 33–35, 40 NLT).

God never allows anything in your life to destroy your faith. Instead, He promises "much praise and glory and honor" for those who allow Him to test and purify them. One day, "it will be worth it all when we see Jesus," as Esther Kerr Rusthoi wrote. "Life's trials will seem so small when we see Christ; one glimpse of His dear face all sorrow will erase, so bravely run the race till we see Christ."*

---

*Esther Kerr Rusthoi, "When We See Christ," © 1941, renewed 1969 Singspiration.

3. Adversity Brings Maturity

The suffering won't last forever.
It won't be long before this generous God
who has great plans for us in Christ—
eternal and glorious plans they are!—
will have you put together and on your feet for good.
1 Peter 5:10 MSG

The message of this verse feels cavalier, at least during times of great trial. Peter's upbeat reminder that God has a glorious plan for His children and will put them back together sounds a bit too good to be true when heartache strips away cheer.

Instead of declaring hope for better times, we're tempted to cry like Job, "It is God who has wronged me" (Job 19:6 NLT). Suffering is hard to understand, especially because God is able to remove it in the blink of an eye. So why doesn't He? We can get lost in the questions of pain. *Is God punishing me? Is this pain simply a result of a fallen world? How can a good God allow such suffering? What should I have done differently?*

When the questions are spent, we come face-to-face with our inability to control life. As suffering continues without relief, we struggle to hope it will last only "a little while." We wonder if we will ever be on our "feet for good."

Job, too, struggled to find hope in the midst of his trials. "Where then is my hope—who can see any hope for me?" he asked (Job 17:15 NIV). Yet this same man who blamed God and struggled to find hope said, "I know that my redeemer lives. . . . I myself will see him with my own eyes—I, and not another. How my heart yearns within me!" (19:25, 27 NIV).

To those in deep waters of suffering, both Job and Peter bring comfort. Job shows that anger and questions coexist with faith. Peter reminds us suffering has an end. The only "forever" for the Christian is the glorious, perfect, joyful eternity with God.

Questions and tears in suffering are okay. Once the emotion is spent, the Christian can say with Habakkuk, "Though the cherry trees don't blossom and the strawberries don't ripen, though the apples are worm-eaten and the wheat fields stunted, though the sheep pens are sheepless and the cattle barns empty, I'm singing joyful praise to GOD. . . . Counting on GOD's Rule to prevail, I take heart and gain strength. I run like a deer" (3:19 MSG).

4. Temporary Troubles

*For our light momentary troubles are achieving for us an
eternal glory that far outweighs them all. So we fix our eyes
not on what is seen, but on what is unseen, since what is
seen is temporary, but what is unseen is eternal.*
2 CORINTHIANS 4:17–18 NIV

Trials. Some are of short duration. But most are long-drawn-out affairs, lasting several weeks, months, or even persisting over interminable years. Some trials are easier to bear than others, while some are extremely intense.

We wonder if we will be able to endure to the end. We wonder if it's worth it, if God even cares. We wonder why we are undergoing the trial. What is the purpose?

Job also questioned God, wondering out loud why God, who had once blessed him with riches, a large family, and prestige, had now turned against him. In the book of the Bible that tells his story, the reader sees right up front why God allowed Satan to rip away all Job's possessions and children and later his health. But Job never knew. And in the end, it didn't matter.

We're told that Job never sinned with his mouth. So even though he had lots of questions, he stated them in a respectful way, truly seeking answers, not in an accusatory or blasphemous manner. In the end, all God would tell him was that Job's perception of God was too small. And in the end God blessed Job with twice the animals and wealth and more children.

We're not told how long Job's trial lasted or how long his friends "blessed" him with their presence and "encouragement" (read discouragement). But that doesn't really matter. Paul told the Corinthian believers that in the light of eternity, our trials here on earth are light (not too heavy for us) and momentary.

Think back to the basics of geometry—a straight line with arrows at each end, indicating infinity. Picture a single pinpoint on that line. That is your life. James calls it a vapor—here today, gone tomorrow. And that is what Paul means when he calls our troubles here on earth momentary.

What a promise! And what encouragement is in this verse. The sum of the troubles we experience here is truly a vapor, the tiniest of pinpoints on the infinite line that is eternity.

5. He Makes a Way of Escape

*No temptation has overtaken you except such as is common
to man; but God is faithful, who will not allow you to be
tempted beyond what you are able, but with the temptation
will also make the way of escape, that you may be able to bear it.*
1 CORINTHIANS 10:13 NKJV

You've been there. Maybe you've even said, "What else could
possibly go wrong?" or "I'm at the end of my rope. I can't handle
anything else." Perhaps you've prayed, "Father, You said . . ." and
then proceeded to remind Him of this promise in 1 Corinthians
10:13. Well-meaning people often quote the platitude, "The Lord
never gives someone more than they can handle," to those who
are going through a difficult trial.

But God does take us beyond the limits of what we believe
we can handle. Maybe that's why the platitude, when applied to
our situation, is hard to hear. Frustration reigns, adding to the
burden, making us wonder if the Lord cares or if He's ignoring
our cries.

Even if our suffering is the result of sin, we long to claim
this promise as our own. But we hesitate, thinking we deserve
whatever God is "dishing out." But that's not what this promise
says. Our way of escape is the Lord in His infinite love pushing
us to make a decision to rely on Him for the strength and
wisdom to walk through the trial He has allowed or to reject His
help and turn away. When we choose to lean on Him, we soon
discover this is His "way of escape."

Linda Bartlett, quoted in the *Bible Promise Book for Women*
(Barbour), says, "Our Creator never intended that we should
shoulder a load of suffering ourselves. That's the whole purpose
of spiritual community." In the same way that God walks with

us through trials, so our local body of believers, whom many call the church "family," will walk beside us: encouraging, praying, helping out in any way they can to lighten the load. Lean on this promise when you feel you are drowning in adverse circumstances. Our faithful God does provide relief from—even a way out of—whatever difficult times He allows.

6. God's Peace Rules

Don't worry about anything; instead, pray about everything.
Tell God what you need, and thank him for all he has done. Then you
will experience God's peace, which exceeds anything we can understand.
His peace will guard your hearts and minds as you live in Christ Jesus.
PHILIPPIANS 4:6–7 NLT

Abigail's marriage to Nabal was probably arranged, as so many
were in those days. Maybe she learned wisdom because of her
marriage to a man who was so aptly named—a fool. But when
she heard of the disaster hanging over her household because
of her husband's latest folly, she acted quickly, boldly, and with
diplomacy. Before destruction could reach her, she sent gifts
and food and drink to those who threatened her home. Then,
without seeking Nabal's approval or permission, she put her plan
into action. She bowed before David, took responsibility for
her husband's actions, and asked David to spare himself from
burdening his conscience with needless bloodshed, praising his
conquests and acknowledging his godly honor and integrity.

She could have sat back and worried and fretted and cried
over her husband's foolish pride that was bringing destruction
on her. She was the victim, not the instigator, after all. She could
have gone to her husband, belittling him with her accusations
and complaints, insisting that he change his mind and do
something before disaster struck. She could have gone to David
and made the same argument her husband had made, pointing
out that there was no contract between him and Nabal. Or she
could have packed her bags and left Nabal, allowing David's
vengeance to fall on her husband alone.

But she didn't. Instead, she took her husband's behavior
before the Lord and listened for His leading.

And in turn, David listened to Abigail, acknowledged the wisdom of her advice, and accepted the gifts she brought. Then she returned home to tell her husband what she had done. Nabal was so angry he had a stroke and died several days later.

God rewarded her choice not to worry and fret by freeing her from a foolish husband and giving her to David to marry. God's peace ruled her heart and mind as she gave Him her worries.

7. God Is with You

David continued to address Solomon: "Take charge! Take heart!
*Don't be anxious or get discouraged. G*od*, my God, is with you in this;*
he won't walk off and leave you in the lurch. He's at your side until
*every last detail is completed for conducting the worship of G*od*.*
You have all the priests and Levites standing ready to pitch in, and
skillful craftsmen and artisans of every kind ready to go to work.
Both leaders and people are ready. Just say the word."
1 Chronicles 28:20–21 msg

Just before David's death, he challenged Solomon, his son
and successor, with the job of building a place of worship, a
permanent dwelling for God in Jerusalem. Years before, David
had wanted to do it, but God, through Nathan His prophet, told
David that he could not build it because David was a man of war
and his hands were bloodstained with the many he had killed
in battle. God instead chose Solomon to do the work and fulfill
David's dream because he would be a man of peace. So David
prepared all the plans and construction drawings—blueprints
with all the specifications, in today's construction language—and
gave them to Solomon.

Solomon looked at the drawings and was filled with anxiety
and consternation at the enormity of the task. He'd never built
anything before, let alone something of this magnitude. It wasn't
even his dream to build a temple for the Lord; it was his father's.
David understood this, but knowing God as he did and knowing
Solomon was God's chosen man, he encouraged his son to
remember all through the project that God would be with him,
directing the construction. Also, all the priests and Levites were
primed to help him. Many of Israel's artisans and builders, and
even one of David's allies, Hiram king of Tyre, were ready to

provide the supplies and labor necessary for building.

Solomon fulfilled his father's dream of building a permanent place to worship God—one of the wonders of the world in his time—and gave God the glory and credit for His continual presence and help (2 Chronicles 6).

When God tasks a person with a project, you can be sure He will equip and enable her to complete the work. It is His promise to everyone He calls.

8. Comfort for Anxious Thinking

When my anxious thoughts multiply within me,
Your consolations delight my soul.
PSALM 94:19 NASB

The word for *anxiety*, or *anxious thoughts*, that the psalmist used in this psalm means to choke or strangle; to harass by tearing, biting, or snapping, especially at the throat; to pull in opposing directions.

That's exactly how someone who is anxious or fretting feels—pulled in too many directions. The enemy loves it when we allow anxiety to rule our thoughts. His main battlefield is the mind, and if he can keep us focused on whatever is causing our anxious thoughts, then he wins that particular skirmish.

But our loving heavenly Father has given us the weapons to fight the enemy of our souls. They are found in His love letter to us.

The verse for today contains the first key—His "consolations," His promises. When you speak His promises out loud, the enemy flees, just as he did when Jesus quoted scripture to counteract Satan's temptations in the wilderness.

Another key in the battle against worry is prayer. In Philippians 4:6, Paul gave specific instructions about the kind of prayer that brings peace and quiet to our souls: "Tell God what you need, and thank him for all he has done" (NLT). *Supplication* is the word used in several Bible versions. It means to make an earnest request; to plead, entreat, intercede. In this kind of prayer we have the help of the Holy Spirit who dwells within us. He knows God's will in every matter, and even when we don't know how to pray about something, He intercedes for us, putting words to our wordless prayers (Romans 8:26–27).

So the next time you feel anxious, pulled in every direction at once, use the keys your gracious Father has provided and rejoice in His answers.

9. No Need for Anxiety

Encourage the exhausted, and make staggering knees firm.
Say to those with an anxious and panic-stricken heart, "Be strong,
fear not! Indeed, your God will come with vengeance [for the
ungodly]; the retribution of God will come, but He will save you."
ISAIAH 35:3–4 AMP

Anxiety weakens our bodies. We're unable to hang on, even to hope. Our brains turn to mush. We can't focus long enough on the problem to come up with a solution. Our muscles weaken. Even our joints weaken until they no longer can hold us upright.

No wonder there are so many research statistics on the effects of long-term stress and anxiety. All of them indicate that many physical, mental, and emotional illnesses are a result of long-term anxiety.

Our culture, instead of dealing with the root causes, develops more and more medications to deal with the symptoms of anxiety. TV and radio commercials focus on medicines that will make us feel better. . .on the surface. These wonder drugs mask the inner pain and fear so we can "enjoy" life, but only God can address the root cause of our anxiety and panic attacks.

The prophet Isaiah wrote and preached in Jerusalem, mainly through Hezekiah's reign, though his life spanned from Hezekiah's grandfather's reign through part of his son's—four kings. Hezekiah faced some very tense moments when he refused to continue paying tribute to Assyria and Egypt. Now the Assyrian army—the same army that had decimated and scattered Israel—was encamped on the plains around Jerusalem. The people panicked. They feared their fate would be the same as that of the other ten tribes. But God sent Isaiah with this message of hope: God was on His way to deliver them with vengeance and retribution.

God kept His promise to exact punishment from the armies and world leaders who would come against His chosen people, against those who were sold out and earnest in serving Him.

God routed the enemy as Judah stood strong in God's strength and courage (see 2 Kings 18–19). And He continues to fight for His people today. Fear not. God will save.

10. No More Pain

"He will wipe every tear from their eyes, and there will be no more death or sorrow or crying or pain. All these things are gone forever."
REVELATION 21:4 NLT

Pain. Sorrow. Death. Violence. Grief. All these are part of life on earth, part of sin's curse brought on when Adam and Eve fell for Satan's deception in the Garden of Eden.

Most of us have sat or stood at the bedside of a loved one or friend wishing we could ease their pain, crying when we said our final good-byes.

Grief is real. . .and hard, even when we know we'll see our loved ones again in heaven. The grief of those who don't have the hope of seeing their loved ones again is even more painful.

A madman—or at least that's how most would describe him—enters a gay bar and mows down the patrons with a semiautomatic assault rifle. We listen in horror as we're told the man claimed an allegiance to ISIS and purposely targeted the bar before the police killed him. We grieve at the number of dead and severely wounded.

Children are kidnapped and sold into slavery or, worse, sexually assaulted, tortured, and finally killed by those who prey on those who aren't able to fight back.

But. . .there is hope and a promise of a better world for those who believe in the ultimate Truth-giver. There is One who took upon Himself the sin of all humankind—the atrocities committed against men, women, and children, the depths of depravity humankind can commit against others—so that we might one day live in an eternity without pain or death or sorrow or crying.

What a wonderful promise to those who receive the free gift of salvation in Jesus Christ alone—one day all our tears will be wiped away, all our pain will be banished, all our grieving over the consequences of sin and death will be forgotten. Forever.

11. The Glorious Rapture

For the Lord himself will come down from heaven, with a loud command, with the voice of the archangel and with the trumpet call of God, and the dead in Christ will rise first. After that, we who are still alive and are left will be caught up together with them in the clouds to meet the Lord in the air. And so we will be with the Lord forever. Therefore encourage one another with these words.
1 THESSALONIANS 4:16–18 NIV

There were many things the believers of the first-century church didn't understand. After Jesus returned to heaven, His disciples were left behind to explain the fundamentals of Christianity, to establish doctrine and practice not only for the Jewish believers but also for the many Gentile believers who were finally able to be included among the chosen people of God.

Paul, a Hebrew of Hebrews, a zealot for the Old Testament Law, was miraculously saved and transformed on the road to Damascus, where he'd been planning to imprison all the "heretics," followers of this New Way. And he became God's primary spokesman for this new entity, the church, made up of those who followed Jesus.

One of the issues that troubled these new believers was what happened to their loved ones after they died. And what did Jesus mean when He said He would return again to take His people to live in heaven with Him forever? Paul addressed these matters in his first letter to the believers in Thessalonica. And what a joyous promise it is even today, twenty-one centuries later.

Jesus indeed is coming for His own. One day soon, we will hear a trumpet blast and the archangel's shout. And for those who have died before us, those whose spirits have gone to be with the Lord, their bodies will rise from the earth to be reunited with their spirits with the Lord. And those of us who are alive will rise to meet the Lord and all those who have gone before us, being forever reunited with each other and with our Lord and Savior.

What a blessed hope! "Even so, come, Lord Jesus" (Revelation 22:20 KJV).

12. The Comforter

*But the Comforter, which is the Holy Ghost, whom the Father
will send in my name, he shall teach you all things, and bring all
things to your remembrance, whatsoever I have said unto you.*
JOHN 14:26 KJV

Jesus promises, "I will not leave you comfortless." Though He
shed His human presence on earth, He dwells with believers
through the Comforter, the Holy Spirit. In the Divine Three-in-
One, the Spirit is separate from Jesus and yet the same. When
talking to His disciples, Jesus explained, "And I will pray the
Father, and he shall give you another Comforter, that he may
abide with you forever; even the Spirit of truth. . .ye know him;
for he dwelleth with you, and shall be in you. I will not leave you
comfortless: I will come to you" (John 14:16–18 KJV).

This same Jesus who never leaves or forsakes His own, who
is with us even unto the end of the world, knows and prays the
Father's plan. He asks that the Spirit of God forever dwells
within believers. This isn't like when the Spirit of God came
"mightily upon" Samson (Judges 14:6 KJV) for a specific task. It is
an indwelling, never-ending, always-there relationship.

What happens in this relationship with the indwelling
God? We are comforted. Instructed. Changed from the inside
out to become more like Jesus. The very Spirit of God Himself
whispers hope in our deepest need, convincing our hearts that
we are indeed God's beloved. The Spirit brings scripture to life,
illuminating truth and making it personal. The Spirit reveals
the character of a God who is loving, joyful, patient, kind, good,
faithful, gentle, and self-controlled. And as He makes His nature
known, He teaches us to reflect it (Galatians 5:22).

Jesus says His sheep know His voice (John 10:4). He speaks

to His chosen through the Holy Spirit, teaching believers to recognize His presence, His guiding hand, His very words.

There is no need to worry about forgetting the things our Lord teaches us. At just the right time and for just the right purpose, our Comforter reminds us of the scriptures we've read, the songs of grace and truth we've sung, and the experiences and lessons the Lord has used to shape our lives. The Spirit blesses us with His ministry of remembrance.

13. The Promise of God's Spirit

"Then I will make up to you for the years that the swarming locust has eaten. . . . You will have plenty to eat and be satisfied and praise the name of the LORD your God, who has dealt wondrously with you. . . . It will come about after this that I will pour out My Spirit upon all mankind; and your sons and daughters will prophesy, your old men will dream dreams, your young men will see visions."
JOEL 2:25–26, 28 NASB

Life on earth is not easy. And Jesus said that before He returned the second time with His armies from heaven, life would be even harder. But at no time will He leave His children without His presence or hope. The prophet Joel spoke and wrote against the southern kingdom of Judah during the time of Joash, several hundred years before the Lord sent Judah into exile. Because of the Israelites' penchant for following after other gods, Judah was experiencing some difficult times. And they were looking forward to even more troubling times if they didn't turn back wholeheartedly to the Lord.

Joel goes on to describe the Day of the Lord, which Bible scholars agree is the final judgment, the Great Tribulation, just before Christ's second coming. In this prophecy, God promises to restore the years the locust—an insect that can decimate crops and plants and trees—has stolen from His people. And He promises the coming of the Holy Spirit, who will comfort His people and dwell within them so they can keep God's law of holiness.

In fact, one of the signs of the end times is a special outpouring of the Spirit on those who are true believers. Sons and daughters will prophesy, old men will dream dreams, and young men will see visions. God's Word will not be replaced.

Instead, these prophecies, dreams, and visions reinforce the presence of the Holy Spirit in times of unprecedented evil and consequent justice.

So as the times get darker and darker and evil seems rampant and uncontrolled, even sanctioned by the world's leaders, look up! The Holy Spirit's ministry will become more apparent as our world grows darker. The return of our Lord is at hand!

14. The Coming Savior

For a child is born to us, a son is given to us. The government will rest on his shoulders. And he will be called: Wonderful Counselor, Mighty God, Everlasting Father, Prince of Peace.
ISAIAH 9:6 NLT

A much-loved tradition at Christmastime is the performance of Handel's *Messiah*, especially those portions that focus on the prophecies surrounding the birth of Jesus Christ. One of the favorites is when the sopranos begin a fugue with the lilting words of Isaiah's prophecy, "For unto us a child is born, unto us a son is given, unto us a son is given." The rest of the choir takes the theme and expands it until the tenors start a new theme and fugue, "And the government will be upon His shoulders." Then the entire chorus comes together in glorious harmony: "And His name shall be called Wonderful, Counselor, the Mighty God, the everlasting Father, the Prince of Peace."

Wonderful Counselor. The first name Isaiah assigns to the Messiah, the Son of God.

How often do we find ourselves in need of wise counsel? Counsel with eternal ramifications?

While God has raised many people over the centuries with the ability to counsel, to give good advice, godly advice, no one does it better than His Son, the Wonderful Counselor. Not only does He direct the Holy Spirit dwelling within us, but He also has given us His written Word, the Bible, the ultimate book of wisdom, advice, and godly counsel.

There is nothing wrong with going to people who give counsel, especially those who give counsel based on the Word of God. But our ultimate Counselor is Jesus Christ. He has promised that if we seek Him, we will find Him (Isaiah 55:6). When we go to Him, He promises to show us great and mighty things that we previously haven't understood or known (Jeremiah 33:3).

Jesus said, "Ask, and it will be given to you; seek, and you will find; knock, and it will be opened to you. For everyone who asks receives, and he who seeks finds, and to him who knocks it will be opened" (Matthew 7:7–8 NASB). And James wrote to encourage believers lacking God's wisdom to ask Him for it, assuring them He would give it to them liberally (James 1:5).

Seek this Wonderful Counselor today. He will be found.

15. Get All the Advice You Can

Get all the advice and instruction you can,
so you will be wise the rest of your life.
PROVERBS 19:20 NLT

Solomon, the wisest man of all time, wrote the book of Proverbs to his son. Grateful to the Lord for giving him the wisdom he had asked for in order to rule His people, Solomon wanted to impart some of his wisdom to his children. Unfortunately, we know from scripture that his son Rehoboam rejected Solomon's fatherly advice. He had no desire to follow the Lord or be guided by Solomon's advisors. And the Lord used his foolishness to divide the kingdom.

However, Solomon's wise words have echoed down through the centuries, and many have profited from them. The verse chosen for this reading emphasizes the importance of getting advice and instruction from others who have learned through experience and the advice of others. In the first chapter of Proverbs, Solomon writes, "The fear of the LORD is the beginning of knowledge" (1:7 NIV). He also advised his son to listen to those who had gone before him, for that is the way of wise men. Foolish men refuse to listen and despise those who try to impart knowledge in an honest effort to help.

When Rehoboam was faced with a major decision right at the beginning of his reign, he made a show of getting advice from the older men, those who had advised Solomon. But instead of heeding their wisdom, he chose to listen to his peers, who were as foolish as he, to his detriment and the detriment of the people.

Giving advice and taking advice are two sides of the same coin. If we are asked to advise someone, we are foolish if we impart advice outside of God's Word, no matter what age we are. To be truly wise in dispensing advice is to give it honestly and then step away, not insisting that those who asked for it follow it. We are not responsible for how others receive it.

Remember, "get all the advice and instruction you can, so you will be wise the rest of your life."

16. The Work of the Holy Spirit

Howbeit when he, the Spirit of truth, is come, he will guide you into all truth; for he shall not speak of himself; but whatsoever he shall hear, that shall he speak: and he will shew you things to come.

JOHN 16:13 KJV

Do you worry about your inability to understand the things of God? Do you fuss about the future—yours or the future of the world? God has not left us in the dark. He gives us the Spirit of truth. The Spirit guides us into truth, helping us make our way through this oft-confusing world.

Luke 24 includes a story of two men, followers of Jesus, who are deeply confused. They've watched the Romans kill the man they believed to be the Messiah. In their grief they heard the rumor that Jesus had come back to life, but such a thing was hard to grasp. As they tried to reason it out, Jesus appeared to them and asked why they were so sad; then, "beginning at Moses and all the prophets, he expounded unto them in all the scriptures the things concerning himself" (Luke 24:27 KJV).

When Jesus gave His disciples the promise of the Spirit of truth, He knew in only a few short hours He would be handed over to the Pharisees and killed. He said, "It is expedient for you that I go away: for if I go not away, the Comforter will not come unto you; but if I depart, I will send him unto you" (John 16:7 KJV).

He wanted to tell them more but knew they weren't able to handle all He had to say. That's when He promised them the Spirit who would guide them into truth and help them navigate the future.

The Lord's heart for His chosen ones is the same today. He knows the world is hurtful and confusing, so He offers Himself to us in the indwelling Spirit of truth. The Spirit knows us better than we know ourselves. When we are able to receive deeper truth, He guides us into what we need to understand. It's His joy to reveal to us the things Jesus wants us to know. Our Lord speaks to us through the Spirit of truth, revealing the mysteries of the spiritual life. He who knows the future leads us by His Spirit, helping us navigate the things to come.

17. No Fear

For God has not given us a spirit of fear and timidity,
but of power, love, and self-discipline.
2 TIMOTHY 1:7 NLT

"Fear not!" is an oft-repeated phrase in scripture. How do you hear it in your head? Is it a command that feels unattainable or a comforting reassurance from the all-powerful God? Scripture tells us not to fear, because our heavenly Father knows we are prone to it. He says not to fear because He always has a plan.

Listen to the comforting words of Isaiah 35:4: "Say to those with fearful hearts, 'Be strong, and do not fear, for your God is coming to destroy your enemies. He is coming to save you'" (NLT).

Fear is a natural human response, but it is not of God. Fear comes from the enemy of our soul. God's perfect love confronts fear, doing away with it. The more we trust Him and His loving plan, the more we live without fear.

God wants to replace our fear and timidity with His love, power, and self-discipline. The Amplified Bible describes personal discipline as "abilities that result in a calm, well-balanced mind and self-control." Don't you love that? What is it like to live with a calm, controlled mind instead of fear?

Because of Jesus' finished work on the cross, we are constantly being transformed from the old human way of thinking and living to His way. Scripture tells us to renew our minds. One way to do this is to meditate on scriptures that replace the old paradigm with the new way of walking in the Spirit with Jesus.

Here's a plan of attack for those who struggle with fear: Read 2 Timothy 1:7 in several versions of the Bible. Pick the one that speaks most deeply to you. Print it on index cards and place one on your mirror and others in your car, your wallet, your refrigerator—wherever you will see them. Memorize this beautiful truth. Think about it. Say it several times a day.

God says He hasn't given us a spirit of fear and timidity. That doesn't mean we never feel afraid, but living by His power does mean standing up to fear. What if the next time fear comes calling you simply answer, "God has not given me a spirit of fear and timidity, but of power, love, and self-discipline"? Try it. Courage is yours for the asking.

18. No Fear, You Are Not Alone

God has said, "I will never fail you. I will never abandon you."
So we can say with confidence, "The LORD is my helper,
so I will have no fear. What can mere people do to me?"
HEBREWS 13:5–6 NLT

"Fear not" or "Do not be afraid" appears 365 times throughout scripture. Humankind is full of fear, but God addresses those fears in His love letter to us.

The Greek word for fear is *phobeo*, the word from which we get our English word *phobia*. Interesting, isn't it? You can Google *phobia* and find lists of fears people have, from ablutophobia (the fear of washing or bathing) to zoophobia (the fear of animals). In fact, there's a whole website dedicated to a complete list of phobias—phobialist.com.

No wonder God has to repeat Himself so many times. Because He is the Creator of all things, there is nothing we need to fear. That doesn't mean we do something foolish like walk off a cliff to prove our lack of fear. The Lord has instilled in us natural fears to prevent us from defying the laws of nature. But excessive fear shows a lack of trust in God. He has told us we don't need to fear, for we are never alone. His presence is always with us in the form of the Holy Spirit who indwells us from the moment we receive God's gift of salvation in Christ alone.

In fact, the writer of Hebrews is quite emphatic in 13:5 when he writes: "I will not in any way fail you nor give you up nor leave you without support. [I will] not, [I will] not, [I will] not in any degree leave you helpless nor forsake nor let [you] down (relax My hold on you)! [Assuredly not!]" (AMPC).

Songwriter Robert Keene picked up on this emphasis when he wrote the following verse of "How Firm a Foundation":

The soul that on Jesus has leaned for repose
I will not, I will not desert to its foes.
That soul, though all hell should endeavor to shake,
I'll never, no, never, no never forsake!

So the next time you are afraid, facing an impossible situation, insurmountable circumstances, or the infernal fires of the enemy, remember you are not alone. The God of the universe, the almighty Creator God, never, ever leaves you alone.

19. No Fear, You Are Safe

"Do not fear, for I have redeemed you; I have summoned you by name;
you are mine. When you pass through the waters, I will be with you;
and when you pass through the rivers, they will not sweep over you.
When you walk through the fire, you will not be burned;
the flames will not set you ablaze."
ISAIAH 43:1–2 NIV

You are Christ's very own. Redeemed by His blood and purchased with His life, you are of great worth. If life turns upside
down, bringing confusion and pain, He is there. When all feels
desperate and looks hopeless, He is with you. He is fully committed to his own.

Old Testament stories mirror New Testament truth.
The Israelites crossed a literal sea and a literal river. Though
both situations looked impossible and the people feared they
would be swept away in waters "uncrossable," God did what
is humanly inconceivable. He cleared a dry path. Not only did
they pass through without drowning; they didn't even have to go
swimming.

And what about Shadrach, Meshach, and Abednego? The
furnace blazed and roared seven times hotter than usual when
they were tossed, bound, into its depths. It was so hot the soldiers
who threw them in were killed. But they walked around in the
fire, completely safe—and, wonders of wonders, they were joined
by a fourth man who looked "like a son of the gods" (Daniel 3:25
NIV). When they were released, they didn't even smell like smoke.

These stories paint a picture for our own comprehension.
When it looks like there is no way out, when troubles seem
poised to sweep us away and we see no way through, God parts
the waters of adversity. When trials blaze, maybe even seven

times hotter than we've ever experienced, we are not alone. The Son of God Himself walks with us, comforting and protecting us, and we are not consumed by the fiery trial.

The promise is true for His chosen ones. He speaks with the same love to ancient Israel and to believers today. "Don't be afraid, I've redeemed you," He says. "I've called your name. You're mine. When you're in over your head, I'll be there with you. When you're in rough waters, you will not go down. When you're between a rock and a hard place, it won't be a dead end" (Isaiah 43:1–2 MSG).

"Do not fear, for I am with you; do not anxiously look about you, for I am your God. I will strengthen you, surely I will help you, surely I will uphold you with my righteous right hand."
ISAIAH 41:10 NASB

Fear. Gut wrenching. Muscle binding. Mind numbing. It's real, and our bodies react to it.

Is God calling you to do something that seems certain to fail? Or maybe the task before you requires you to climb higher by faith than you have ever climbed before. . .and there's no safety net below. At least none that you can see. Or is He stretching your faith and asking you to walk a path you can't see? You have no idea where the pitfalls are, though you know they must be there. And the only light you have is so small you can't see more than one step ahead.

It's a scary place to be. An exhilarating one.

How can a situation be both at one time? It is scary, mind-numbingly frightening, in fact, if we look at it with our earthly eyes. But it is also exhilarating if we look at the opportunity through the eyes of faith, knowing God is with us every step of the way.

The people of Israel were facing judgment from God because of their continued insistence on going their own way. Exile—away from the land God had given them, away from all that was known—at the hands of the new world power, the Babylonians, was a very real threat. But God gave them this promise: "You have no need to fear what is ahead. You don't need to look around you at all the potential dangers. I'm your God. I will strengthen you for the hard journey ahead. I will help you with every step you take. I will hold you up—and you will stand strong—with my righteous right hand of power" (author's paraphrase).

God is all-powerful, all-knowing, and always present. Always. We can step forward into whatever the future holds without fear.

21. Guard Your Heart

Guard your heart above all else,
for it determines the course of your life.
Proverbs 4:23 NLT

In the tone of a wise, caring father, the author of Proverbs 4 appeals to readers to take his counsel "to heart." He offers a *heart*felt plea for the reader to "get wisdom" and "develop good judgment." He contrasts this with wicked living that "is like total darkness" where evildoers "have no idea what they are stumbling over" (Proverbs 4:5, 19 NLT). Our choices *do* have consequences. When we act with good judgment, taking wisdom *to heart*, there are good results. But what happens when we make decisions without seeking wisdom first? Stumbling and "total darkness."

In the midst of this plea to pursue wisdom, the author admonishes, "Above all else, guard your heart, for everything you do flows from it" (4:23 NIV). The New American Standard Bible says the very "springs of life" flow from the heart.

A heart must be guarded because it needs protection! Unwise decisions, whether our own or those thrust upon us by unwise or wicked people, have wounding consequences. The heart is hurt when its affections are set on worldly ambitions or unhealthy relationships. One of the most serious, life-altering assaults upon hearts is false belief.

False belief systems often result from the wounding the heart endures, and they are full of insidious lies. The enemy works to kill life-issuing hearts by whispering that God's people are unlovable, inadequate, powerless, and unworthy of the blessings God has already given. The enemy's design is destruction. He fights to keep us from the life Jesus gave—a life that is full and abundant (John 10:10)!

Jesus contradicts the lies with the cross—His sacrifice proving His creation is loved, His blood making us worthy, and His Spirit empowering wholesome, meaningful living. When lies assault our heart, we stand guard by living in the truth of the cross.

Protecting the heart is tricky business. Sometimes we must give up unhealthy affections. Other times we must walk away from relationships that assault our hearts. We have to maintain constant vigilance to reject lies and believe the truth. Always we must seek God's wisdom and take it *to heart*.

22. Make Certain of His Calling

Applying your diligence [to the divine promises, make every effort]
in [exercising] your faith to, develop moral excellence, . . .knowledge
(insight, understanding), . . .self-control, . . .steadfastness, . . .godliness,
. . .brotherly affection, and. . .[develop Christian] love [that is, learn to
unselfishly seek the best for others and to do things for their benefit]. . . .
Therefore, believers, be all the more diligent to make certain about
His calling and choosing you [be sure that your behavior reflects
and confirms your relationship with God]; for by doing these things
[actively developing these virtues], you will never stumble [in your
spiritual growth and will live a life that leads others away from sin].
2 PETER 1:5–7, 10 AMP

Several places in both Paul's and Peter's writings we see them
encouraging their readers to "make certain" of God's calling. In
this passage in 2 Peter, Peter encourages believers to be diligent
in applying the promises of God to our spiritual walk with
Christ. For when we do, others see Christ and are attracted to
this way of life.

Another benefit of taking hold of God's promises is that we
become stronger and stronger in our personal faith, and we no
longer have the tendency to stumble over our own sin or to cause
others to stumble over us.

The idea of practicing diligence or exercising our faith
muscles to develop Christian character can be expressed in
a musical term—to chorus together. In other words, moral
excellence, knowledge, self-control, steadfastness, godliness,
brotherly affection, and love aren't just slapped together one on
top of the other to create a whole. Rather, they are "chorused"
together into a harmonious whole.

For a musical composition, the composer may have a single

melody in mind. But as it is developed, other lines are developed and woven together into a pleasant-sounding arrangement. All the parts work together, with one part taking precedence at times, then another. But in the end all those parts merge into a piece that is complete and full.

God desires Christian character to perform as a complete symphony, with each of His promises forming a harmony with the melody that is pleasing to everyone who experiences it.

23. Don't Despair

*So let's not get tired of doing what is good. At just the right
time we will reap a harvest of blessing if we don't give up.*
GALATIANS 6:9 NLT

If anyone had a right to get tired of doing good, it was Joseph.
As a teenager (probably age seventeen), he was given a dream of
greatness. How he must have anticipated the power and honor
that would be his!

But what happened over the next several years looked very
different. First Joseph's brothers sold him into slavery. His life
became a cycle. Joseph worked hard, gained favor, then was
mistreated. Through no fault of his own, he eventually found
himself in an Egyptian prison. Joseph was thirty years old before
he experienced the fulfillment of the prophecy. No doubt those
thirteen years felt like an eternity to young Joseph!

But Joseph didn't waste those years. He lived with integrity
and did good wherever life took him. Joseph lived out the admonition Paul later gave the church at Galatia: "Pay careful attention
to your own work, for then you will get the satisfaction of a job
well done. . . . We are each responsible for our own conduct"
(Galatians 6:4–5 NLT).

Joseph could have responded differently to the pain he
experienced, but he chose to live according to God's ways.
Eventually he harvested much good, not only in his own life, but
also in the lives of those he helped. Paul said, "You will always
harvest what you plant. Those who live only to satisfy their own
sinful nature will harvest decay and death. . . . But those who live
to please the Spirit will harvest everlasting life from the Spirit"
(6:7–8 NLT).

It isn't easy in life's waiting room. God often gives dreams long before He fulfills them. Sometimes years, not months, pass. Waiting is difficult, but it is our training ground. Like Joseph, we have a choice to make. We can live to please the Spirit of God in the waiting, looking to Him for a good harvest, or we can become bitter and give up on doing good.

For those who stay the course, there *will* be a harvest. It may not look exactly as we dreamed. Joseph likely didn't expect to end up second in command to Pharaoh! But God promises that at just the right time, the harvest comes.

24. Your Work Is Not in Vain

Therefore, my beloved brethren, be steadfast, immovable,
always abounding in the work of the Lord,
knowing that your labor is not in vain in the Lord.
1 CORINTHIANS 15:58 NKJV

We've all been there at one time or another. Many of us multiple times. In over our heads. Frustrated. Tired. No, more than that, exhausted from too many sleepless nights. Discouraged. Ready to quit. Alone. Facing the giants with hardly enough strength to lift an eyebrow, let alone the body armor we need to survive.

Statistics say that most people quit within days, hours, minutes of breakthrough. How sad! To be so close to victory, to success, and then quit. Comparatively, only a few persevere and push through to the end. No one remembers a person who gave up, but everyone hears about the one who perseveres through all the difficulties to realize a dream.

Paul, at the end of a long discussion of the Gospel— Jesus Christ's death, burial, and resurrection—encourages the Corinthian believers not to give up on the Christian life too soon. We need to be steadfast, unmoving from our position in Christ, pushing through to the end. And sometimes the only way we can find the strength to continue on is to remember that nothing we do for the Lord is in vain. It isn't empty, good-for-nothing works that move us forward. Knowing our work is for the Lord, the Creator God of the universe, gives everything we do meaning and purpose.

Paul feared being put on a shelf for doing nothing to promote the Word, for beating the air to no avail. And he didn't want that for those who followed him. He didn't want them to fall short of receiving their reward in heaven. So at the end of his reasoned discussion of why the Gospel isn't vain or empty, he penned these words of encouragement, of promise: nothing we do for the Lord is empty or to no purpose. Even if we don't understand everything now, one day we will.

Ralph Waldo Emerson said, "Whatever course you decide upon, there is always someone to tell you that you are wrong. There are always difficulties arising which tempt you to believe that your critics are right. To map out a course of action and follow it to an end requires courage."

So keep on keeping on. Push through to the end. . .with God's ever-present help and courage.

25. Suffering That Brings Glory

We now have this light shining in our hearts, but we ourselves
are like fragile clay jars containing this great treasure. . . .
We are pressed on every side by troubles, but we are not crushed.
We are perplexed, but not driven to despair. We are hunted down,
but never abandoned by God. We get knocked down, but we are
not destroyed. Through suffering, our bodies continue to share in the
death of Jesus so that the life of Jesus may also be seen in our bodies.
2 Corinthians 4:7–10 NLT

Let's be honest: Life is hard. We get knocked down. We are
hunted. It seems we have targets on our backs and expert archers
are aiming for the bull's-eye. Troubles press us in on every side,
threatening to squeeze us flat in the vise of life. Our bodies are
fragile, and even the smallest pebble lobbed our way is a boulder
that will crush us.

Paul says that even though our lives are like fragile clay
jars, the problems that press in on us do not crush us. We take a
tumble, but we're not completely shattered. Wicked people hunt
us down, wanting to destroy everything Christlike in us.

But God never leaves us to fight alone. We're not crushed by
the troubles that press us facedown in the dirt of the filthy world
system. Even though life is perplexing and we can't fathom God's
purposes for our lives, we're not driven to despair. We will get
knocked down, but we're never out for long. God is in our corner
and pulls us back up, holding us until we're steady.

Why does He allow the hardships of life?

Because as we suffer for Christ, we are strengthened and
made indestructible with the same power that raised Him from
the dead. His light and power shine in and through us.

What a wonderful promise! No matter how hard life gets,

the Lord is continually making us stronger in order to face a world system and its dark prince whose only purpose is to destroy us so that Christ's light cannot be seen.

Paul says it this way in his letter to the Romans: "If God is for us, who can be against us?" (8:31 NKJV). The answer: No one!

26. Godly Discipline Yields Peaceable Fruit

No discipline is enjoyable while it is happening—it's painful!
But afterward there will be a peaceful harvest of right living
for those who are trained in this way.
HEBREWS 12:11 NLT

As children never look forward to discipline from their parents, so believers don't desire discipline from God, their loving heavenly Father. However, even children recognize the importance of discipline.

A wise teenager thanked his parents for applying the "board of education" to his "seat of knowledge" after a discussion of a student who was going through a very rough time of discipline at school. The second teenager's parents hadn't learned the importance of discipline when their child was young, and making up for lost time now was tough on all of them.

Was discipline any nicer for the first teenager whose parents had disciplined him when he was a young boy? No. And he admits it may have taken him longer than most children to finally "get" it, but he did and life was much easier in the end. And his teen years were a joy. But until we become adults with our own children to discipline, we don't really understand how hard discipline is—good, consistent, godly discipline.

Then we better understand God's discipline. Puritan theologian Stephen Charnock wrote, "We often learn more of God under the rod that strikes us than under the staff that comforts us." God promises that after a time of discipline—a time when He purges sin and ungodly behaviors from us— our life will yield a peaceful harvest of right living. And what a blessed peace that is! It is far beyond our understanding

(Philippians 4:7). It wraps us in a warm blanket of comfort. It spills from within us until others are affected by it and desire it for themselves.

Be patient during your time of discipline. And be patient with others who may be a part of your discipline. God can use anything and anyone as tools to sharpen us, strengthen us, and secure us as one of His own. If you are undergoing discipline, rejoice! It is proof that you are a true child of God. He lovingly purges you of behaviors that stunt your spiritual growth. He loves you too much to allow you to continue in behaviors that will bring harm to you and to His people.

27. God's Correction

"Behold, how happy is the man whom God reproves, so do not despise the discipline of the Almighty. For He inflicts pain, and gives relief; He wounds, and His hands also heal."
JOB 5:17–18 NASB

When trouble descended on Job, several of his friends came to commiserate with him. . .and to help him see why God was punishing him. At least they thought they were being helpful. The author of Job says his friends initially sat in silence with him for several days.

But there were times in the following days, once they allowed their tongues free rein, when Job complained they were no comfort at all. Yet in the midst of expressing their own righteousness and false assumptions, they sometimes spoke a nugget of truth.

Eliphaz was the first of Job's friends to speak. Near the end of his first "speech," he tells Job not to despise God's discipline. In Eliphaz's mind, God was punishing Job for some undisclosed, secret sin. Of course we learn later that God rejected Eliphaz's assessment of the situation and had Job pray for forgiveness for Eliphaz and his other three friends.

At one point in Job's ordeal, he says he wishes there was some gross sin he could repent of so that he could see the purpose of his suffering, but there isn't. He doesn't despise God's discipline, for he understands the end result of godly discipline is happiness and blessings from God.

Job was right in believing that godly discipline purges us of unrighteous living. Part of his daily prayers involved intercession on behalf of his children because of the potential that their many parties included ungodly behaviors. But he could think of no reason for God's discipline at that time in his life. Still, Eliphaz hit on an eternal truth. We are blessed when God reproves us, for His discipline is a proof of our place in His family. As Elisabeth Elliot wrote, "God has to punish his children from time to time, and it is the very demonstration of His love."

28. Many Mansions

"My Father's house has many rooms; if that were not so, would I have told you that I am going there to prepare a place for you? And if I go and prepare a place for you, I will come back and take you to be with me that you also may be where I am."
JOHN 14:2–3 NIV

Christian bookstores have sold many journals over the years. One day a godly grandmother, knowing she might not be around much longer, picked up a journal titled *A Journal of Faith and Love: Grandmother's Memories to Her Grandchild* and filled out the journal prompts for her eldest grandchild when she graduated from high school.

Many years passed, and her granddaughter discovered the journal among her things as she was packing to move. As she reread the journal, the entries took on new meaning. One entry stood out.

"When I die, I believe that I will go directly to be with the Lord," wrote her grandmother in her beautiful cursive. "In 2 Corinthians 5:6–9, Paul discusses this, saying that we know this by faith, not by sight. However, I vividly remember my Grandma Fields telling us about her mother's death. She said she had been nearly in a coma, but suddenly sat upright and cried, 'Look! I see ___ and ___ [children who had died young]! And I see Jesus!' "

When she read this, the granddaughter recalled that just before her grandma died, she, too, saw a vision of heaven, seeing many of her family and friends who had gone on before her. The young woman had been present and heard her grandma describe the people and the place as well as she could with halting breath. Hampered by the lack of words to describe the colors and other beautiful things she saw, her grandma kept saying, "It's so much more! There are no words."

Heaven, and the promise of the eternal home Jesus went to prepare for us, became even more precious and real to that young woman not only the day of her grandma's vision, but also the day she rediscovered the journal. Heaven is real, and one day our eternal home will be ready for us as Jesus promised, and He will come to take us home.

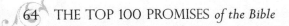

29. Death Produces Life

"I tell you the truth, unless a kernel of wheat is planted in the
soil and dies, it remains alone. But its death will produce
many new kernels—a plentiful harvest of new lives."
JOHN 12:24 NLT

Death. It seems final, but it is simply an entry to new life. When Jesus talked about the kernel of wheat that must die before it produces a harvest, He prophesied of His death on the cross. Because He offered His sinless life in sacrifice, He opened the way for anyone who believes in Him to receive a new life here on this earth as well as everlasting life for eternity.

Though Jesus is fully God, He was also fully man, with all the emotions and struggles of the human condition. After foretelling His imminent death, He said, "Now my soul is deeply troubled. Should I pray, 'Father, save me from this hour'? But this is the very reason I came! Father, bring glory to your name" (John 12:27–28 NLT).

Death brings pain—it even brought pain to Jesus Himself. As He faced His greatest trial, He clung to His call to reconcile a sinful people back to their Creator and to glorify His Father. Jesus stood firmly committed to His Father's plan, but that doesn't mean He didn't struggle to surrender to it. In the scripture above, we hear hints of His impending battle to choose His Father's will over His own. It was no easy war He fought with Himself in the Garden of Gethsemane. In fact, scripture says He prayed so hard He sweat drops of blood.

The good news is Jesus didn't only set a pattern for surrender to death; He also resurrected! Just as Jesus rose from the grave and drew the world back to God, He resurrects our passions, dreams, and ministries. When He does, we discover they have a new purity, shining with the anointing oil of the Holy Spirit. Our battle to surrender and to lie buried for a season teaches us more about our Lord and more about ourselves. Our capacity to surrender to the One who has asked us to die that we might live has expanded. We are ready now to enter our destiny and reap the harvest He planned all along.

30. The Promised New Heavens and New Earth

But in accordance with His promise we expectantly await
new heavens and a new earth, in which righteousness dwells.
2 PETER 3:13 AMP

Peter wrote his second epistle shortly before he was martyred
for the sake of the Gospel. He knew his time on earth was short,
so in this letter to believers undergoing persecution, he wanted
to remind them of Jesus' promises of life after death, or life after
Jesus' second coming in the air to take His children home.

Because of the persecution of believers that heated up
during Nero's reign as emperor, many doubters and false teachers
questioned Jesus' claim to return again. Many believers had died
in the years since Jesus' ascension into heaven, including many
who had died in the various persecutions. These false teachers
and doubters said that everything was still going on as it had
since the creation.

But Peter recalled Jesus' words during His teaching ministry
on earth about a final judgment to come. The judgment by a
universal flood in Noah's time came when people didn't believe
in Noah's prophecy of coming destruction. So will the final
judgment of fire also come just as Jesus prophesied. But Peter
reminded his readers that not only would the old heaven and
earth be destroyed by fire, but a new heaven and a new earth
would be created.

John describes the new heaven (new Jerusalem) and the new
earth coming as "a bride beautifully dressed for her husband"
(Revelation 21:2 NLT). Then Jesus will say, "Look, I am making
everything new!" (21:5 NLT). Jesus also went on to say about
those who will inhabit the new earth, "It is finished! I am the

Alpha and the Omega—the Beginning and the End. To all who are thirsty I will give freely from the springs of the water of life. All who are victorious will inherit all these blessings, and I will be their God, and they will be my children" (21:6–7 NLT).

Just as Jesus promised He would return for the final judgment, He promised He would prepare a new heaven and a new earth for those who accept His gift of salvation, of righteousness, in Christ alone.

So take heart. Don't be discouraged. God has promised us an eternity in heaven. He hasn't forgotten.

31. Reap Eternal Life

Those who live only to satisfy their own sinful nature will harvest decay and death from that sinful nature. But those who live to please the Spirit will harvest everlasting life from the Spirit.
GALATIANS 6:8 NLT

The principle of sowing and reaping is an eternal truth. In the verse before this, Paul wrote, "Whatever a man sows, this he will also reap" (6:7 NASB). Jesus told several parables that illustrate this principle.

When a sower went out to sow seed, it fell on various kinds of ground. "Some seeds fell beside the road, and the birds came and ate them up. Others fell on the rocky places, where they did not have much soil; and immediately they sprang up. . . . But when the sun had risen, they were scorched; and because they had no root, they withered away. Others fell among the thorns, and the thorns came up and choked them out. And others fell on the good soil and yielded a crop" (Matthew 13:4–8 NASB). Later when He explained the parable to His disciples, He compared the seed to the Word of God being sown in various types of hearts and described the end results (13:19–23).

At another time He talked about good seed and bad seed, good fruit and bad fruit, and how each produced after its kind (see Matthew 12:33; Luke 6:43).

Paul wrote to the churches in Galatia, wondering at how quickly they had allowed false doctrine to slip into their teaching. And again the principle of sowing and reaping entered the discussion. He reminded them that whatever they sowed in life—things that gave pleasure to the flesh or worldly appetites or things that were of the Spirit of God—they would reap in death. So those who live only for themselves, to please themselves, will harvest decay and eternal death. Those who live to please the Holy Spirit will harvest eternal life in heaven with the Lord.

What we do here on earth matters. As Moses urged the children of Israel to choose life as they settled into the Promised Land (Deuteronomy 30:15–20), so Paul urged his readers to choose life, eternal life, while still here on earth. Before it's too late. Eternity is real.

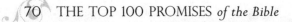

32. We Will Never Die

Jesus said to [Martha], "I am the resurrection and the life;
he who believes in Me will live even if he dies,
and everyone who lives and believes in Me will never die."
JOHN 11:25–26 NASB

Mary, Martha, and Lazarus were special friends of Jesus. They always had a place for Him and His disciples to stay whenever they came through Bethany, a small town near Jerusalem. They provided a comfortable place to sleep and good food to eat.

One day Jesus got word that Lazarus was very sick and was expected to die. But Jesus didn't rush to his friend's bedside right away. Instead, He stayed where He was, much to the bewilderment of His disciples. A few days later, He received word of Lazarus's death, but He told His disciples He was ready to go to Lazarus because now "he slept." Again the disciples were puzzled. Wasn't it a good sign that he slept? Didn't that mean he was getting better? Why did they need to go now?

Jesus then stated baldly, "He's dead," which only added to the disciples' confusion. By this time, most had figured out that Jesus had a lesson to teach them.

But Martha and Mary weren't so understanding. Both reproached Jesus when He finally arrived, saying that if only He had been there, Lazarus would still be alive.

In Jesus' conversation with Martha, He reminded her that Lazarus would live again. When Martha remarked that she knew one day Lazarus would be resurrected, Jesus spoke these words of truth and life to her: "I am the resurrection and the life; he who believes in Me will live even if he dies, and everyone who lives and believes in Me will never die."

Soon she, too, understood the truth of His words, especially after He raised Lazarus from the dead and restored him to his sisters.

Jesus' promise of eternal life is for those who believe and receive His free gift of salvation. They may die a physical death, but they will live eternally with Him in heaven.

Jesus raised Lazarus from physical death. But though Lazarus experienced a second physical death, he never experienced eternal death. We will see him among the saints in heaven and spend eternity with him.

33. What Is Faith?

*The fundamental fact of existence is that this trust in God,
this faith, is the firm foundation under everything that
makes life worth living. It's our handle on what we can't see.*
HEBREWS 11:1 MSG

What is faith? An age-old question. Hebrews 11:1 gives
us a definition for the noun form: it is the firm foundation
under everything that makes life worth living. We can't see
a foundation. It's buried deep in the ground. But it is there,
providing the support we need for a building, for a life.

But faith isn't just a noun. It's also a verb, an active verb.

One helpful definition is that faith is believing God even
when He doesn't make sense, humanly speaking, and obeying
Him no matter what.

Scripture often admonishes us to walk by faith, not by sight.
But what does that mean?

Abraham is the quintessential example of one who lived by
faith. Paul tells us, "Abraham believed God, and it was counted
unto him for righteousness" (Romans 4:3 kjv). God came to
Abraham in a vision and restated the promises He had made
earlier: Abram would be the father of a great nation, innumerable
as the stars; his seed, the promised son, would come through
Sarai, his wife; he and his descendants would have the land
where he now lived as a stranger. Then Abram believed God—
that He would keep His promises—and God counted it to him
as righteousness (see Genesis 15:1–6).

Abraham confronted his ultimate test of faith when Isaac,
the son of promise, was a teenager (see Genesis 22). God told
Abraham to sacrifice Isaac on an altar. Scripture doesn't tell us
whether Abraham argued; it just says that he rose early in the

morning the next day and took Isaac and several servants on a three-day journey to the mountain God had specified. Once there, Isaac allowed his father to bind him and lay him on top of the wood on the altar. But just as Abraham raised his arm to plunge the knife into Isaac's breast, God stopped him. He was satisfied that Abraham's faith in Him was strong and active.

In Hebrews 11:19 we're told Abraham believed that if God let him go through with killing the promised son, He was able to raise him from the dead.

Faith in action—may we all exhibit this kind of faith, being obedient even when we do not understand.

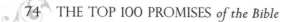

34. Hopeless? Believe God Anyway

*When everything was hopeless, Abraham believed anyway,
deciding to live not on the basis of what he saw he couldn't do but
on what God said he would do. . . . Abraham didn't focus on his
own impotence and say, "It's hopeless. This hundred-year-old body
could never father a child." Nor did he survey Sarah's decades of
infertility and give up. He didn't tiptoe around God's promise
asking cautiously skeptical questions. He plunged into the promise
and came up strong, ready for God, sure that God would make
good on what he had said. That's why it is said, "Abraham was
declared fit before God by trusting God to set him right."*

ROMANS 4:18–22 MSG

It's not easy to believe in something we can't see. Yet Abraham,
at seventy-five years, heard God tell him to leave the land where
he'd been born and raised and lived and travel to a country that
God would show him. And Abraham packed up his household,
took his wife and nephew (and initially his father, Terah),
and set out to obey. After a stop in Haran where Terah died,
Abraham resumed his journey to this land only God knew
(Genesis 11:27–12:9).

God had also promised to make Abraham the father of a
great, innumerable nation through a son who would be born to
Sarah. He laughed and so did Sarah, not totally in unbelief, but
in incredulity that God would wait until he was one hundred and
Sarah ninety before giving them Isaac (Genesis 17:17; see also
Genesis 15, 21).

Scripture tells us in several places that Abraham believed
God's promises, even when they took a long time to fulfill. Paul
says in this passage in Romans 4 that Abraham hoped even when
the circumstances dictated there was no hope. He didn't focus

on his old body, but instead he placed his faith in the God who could make it happen.

What about you? Has God made promises to you? Scholars say there are over five thousand promises in the Word of God. And they are all for us! How is your faith—believing or unbelieving? If Abraham, another mortal like us, believed God was able to keep His promises to him, how much more should we believe the same, no matter the impossibilities surrounding the promises? As children of God, believers in Jesus Christ, let us be obedient to the voice of the Spirit when He urges us to "walk by faith, not by sight."

35. Little Seed, Big Faith

*And the Lord said, "If you had faith like a mustard seed,
you would say to this mulberry tree, 'Be uprooted and
be planted in the sea'; and it would obey you."*
LUKE 17:6 NASB

Mustard seed is the smallest of all herb seeds. Insignificant, miniscule, easily scattered—these words aren't indicative of the large shrubs that result from the tiny seeds.

Jesus said that if we have faith even as small as the smallest herb seed He created, we can move mountains (Matthew 17: 20). In other words, anything we believe He *can* do He *will* if we ask in faith.

Peter tested this promise when Jesus came walking on water in the middle of a storm to where the disciples were trying to keep their small boat from capsizing. Once they knew who the "ghost" was, Peter asked to walk on water, too.

Jesus invited him to come, and Peter stepped out of the boat and walked a few steps on the water. As long as he kept his eyes on Jesus, all was well. But as soon as he took his eyes off Jesus and looked at the tempestuous sea around him, he panicked and started to sink. But before he could more than cry out, "Lord, save me!" Jesus reached out His hand, grabbed hold of Peter, and calmed the stormy sea. Once they had climbed into the boat, He turned to Peter and said, "You are with the One who created all things, the One who sustains all things—why did you doubt?" (See Matthew 14.)

The same question echoes down through the centuries since then: Why do you doubt?

Faith is essential for a vibrant relationship with Christ. In Hebrews 11:6 we read, "It's impossible to please God apart from faith. And why? Because anyone who wants to approach God must believe both that he exists *and* that he cares enough to respond to those who seek him" (msg). If we believe God enough to accept His free gift of salvation in Christ alone, then why can't we believe Him for everything else?

Even a little faith accomplishes much when we believe and act on His promises.

36. Full Rights and Privileges

*For you [who are born-again have been reborn from above—
spiritually transformed, renewed, sanctified and] are all
children of God [set apart for His purpose with full rights
and privileges] through faith in Christ Jesus.*
GALATIANS 3:26 AMP

Growing up is confusing. If you're looking to rules and privileges
to know when you're an adult, you can drive at sixteen. At
eighteen you can vote and die for your country. Other privileges
come at twenty-one, but parents can claim you as a child on their
health insurance until you're twenty-six.

It's not like that with Jesus. To claim full rights and privileges
as a child of God, you need only one thing—His salvation. There
is no coming of age, no maturity hoops to jump through. Jesus
did it all when He reconciled us to His Father and established us
as His coheirs.

As God's children we are no longer in bondage to the
darkness of this world. We are free to enjoy a life of grace,
without guilt and shame. As His beloved children, we're seated
with Jesus at the right hand of our Father, the King of kings!

Earlier in this chapter, Paul rebukes the Galatians. They're
looking to their behavior and to the law for righteousness. He
says that all who seek "justification and salvation by obedience
to the Law and the observance of rituals" live under a curse (3:10
AMP). The law was given to reveal sin but can never solve sin's
problems.

The Galatians chose to live beneath the authority of a tutor
instead of living as free and mature citizens of heaven. It's easy
to be aghast at their choice. Who would give up the wonder of
living with God as a personal Father, who bestows all the rights

and privileges of heaven upon His children?

But don't we slip into the same thinking?

We stumble and are ashamed. Soon we live as unworthy, as if we're in prison instead of the throne room of heaven. Or we focus on good behavior or service, trying to gain God's favor by what we *do* instead of realizing we already have it because of who we *are*. We trade a personal, vibrant relationship of unconditional love for a list of standards.

Thankfully it doesn't have to be this way! As children of the Father, purchased by the blood of Jesus, we *always* have full access into the family room and our heavenly Daddy's heart!

37. Anything Is Possible

"What do you mean, 'If I can'?" Jesus asked.
"Anything is possible if a person believes."
MARK 9:23 NLT

This poor father, barely hanging on by a thread, brought his troubled son to Jesus. The boy was possessed by a very strong demon, one who delighted in putting the boy in harm's way. At the demon's will the boy would fall into a fit or a seizure, making him mute. "Whenever [the evil spirit] seizes him," his father told Jesus, "it slams him to the ground and he foams at the mouth, and grinds his teeth and stiffens out. . . . It has often thrown him both into the fire and into the water to destroy him" (Mark 9:18, 22 NASB). His father was weary from having to keep an eye on his son 24/7.

But he didn't find Jesus, only His disciples. Jesus had taken James, John, and Peter, His inner circle, up the mountain, where He was transfigured and met with Moses and Elijah. The remaining disciples tried to heal the boy, but nothing happened.

Frustrated, exhausted, at his wit's end, the father approached Jesus as soon as He came down the mountain. At this point, the faith and hope that had brought him to seek healing for his son had faded almost into nothing. His words to Jesus reflect his extreme disappointment: "If You can, will You heal my son?"

Jesus replied, "If I can? Anything is possible if a person believes." And He healed the boy, casting out the demon.

Later, the disciples asked Jesus why they couldn't cast out that demon. Jesus said, "This kind can be cast out only by prayer" (Mark 9:28–29 NLT).

How about you? Are you facing an impossible situation today? Are you weary of trying to make it work? Of fixing it?

Remember, anything is possible if a person believes.

As the old chorus by Eugene Clark reminds us, "Nothing is impossible when you put your trust in God. Nothing is impossible when you're trusting in His Word. Hearken to the voice of God to thee: 'Is there anything too hard for Me?' Then put your trust in God alone and rest upon His Word. For everything, O everything, yes, everything is possible with God."

38. Keep Your Eyes on Jesus

Keep your eyes on Jesus, who both began and finished this race
we're in. Study how he did it. Because he never lost sight of where
he was headed—that exhilarating finish in and with God—he could
put up with anything along the way: Cross, shame, whatever.
And now he's there, in the place of honor, right alongside God.
When you find yourselves flagging in your faith, go over that story
again, item by item, that long litany of hostility he plowed through.
That will shoot adrenaline into your souls!
HEBREWS 12:2–3 MSG

Imagine heaven's grandstands. There are Joshua and Esther. Between them stands your grandma, and your best friend is next to her. But who is that, right in the middle? The one cheering most loudly, practically jumping with excitement? It's none other than Jesus Himself. You fix your eyes upon His radiant face. The weariness fades. You stop wondering if you were meant to win or even run. You believe victory is yours.

Hebrews 12 compares the Christian life to a race requiring great endurance. The Father sets the path, and it is Jesus, already a champion, who creates winners. Not only does His blood give victory, but His example helps His chosen ones endure hardship, let go of shame, and never give up.

But He doesn't stop there. He who initiated faith perfects it.

A common technique in driver's education is to teach students to look where they want the car to go if their car starts sliding. If the driver looks toward the slide, that's where the car goes, but if he focuses on the road in front of him, the car rights itself.

Isn't the Christian walk like that? If we keep our eyes on Jesus, we go where He leads. We become like Him. We find courage. But if we focus on entangling sins, we slip back into them. If we focus on faults and failures, we repeat them. If we focus on obstacles we lose heart.

We have a promise: our Lord will perfect our faith. It's not our job to worry about whether we can run this race. We simply keep our focus on the One who has already won. He leads us to victory.

39. Faithful to All Generations

"Understand, therefore, that the LORD your God is indeed God.
He is the faithful God who keeps his covenant for a thousand
generations and lavishes his unfailing love on those
who love him and obey his commands."
DEUTERONOMY 7:9 NLT

Throughout scripture and throughout history we can see God's faithfulness to His people, to His Word, and to His nature. Even when the circumstances are the darkest and the most impossible humanly speaking, God's faithfulness to keep His people, to provide for them, to protect them, to fight for them, to fulfill every promise He ever made is evident.

In the book of Deuteronomy, we read Moses' final summation of all that had happened to the children of Israel to that point. They were on the verge of finally entering the Promised Land, and Moses didn't want them to forget God's faithfulness to them in spite of their many failings and times of unbelief.

Like Moses, Jeremiah also reminded God's people of His great faithfulness. In the first chapter of the book that bears his name, we read how Jeremiah, also known as the weeping prophet, received his call from the Lord. God told him to go to the people of Judah and proclaim His message to them. He told Jeremiah the people would not listen and would make his life miserable as a result. Not an encouraging prospect for a newly ordained prophet.

Jeremiah's life was not easy. He was mocked, ignored, put in prison. The scroll in which he wrote all God's words to His people in the last days before their exile in Babylon was burned, section by section, by the king of Judah himself! No wonder he earned the name of the weeping prophet.

The book of Lamentations is hard reading since it records Jeremiah's reasons for his tears. Chapter 3 chronicles his feelings over the destruction of Jerusalem because of the sin of the people. But in the middle of his honest assessment of his feelings, he writes: "This I recall to my mind, therefore have I hope. It is of the LORD's mercies that we are not consumed, because his compassions fail not. They are new every morning: great is thy faithfulness" (Lamentations 3:21–23 KJV).

When life is most difficult, follow Moses' and Jeremiah's example, and look for God's mercies and faithfulness in everything.

40. Formed in Secret

For You did form my inward parts; You did knit me together in my mother's womb. I will confess and praise You for You are fearful and wonderful and for the awful wonder of my birth! Wonderful are Your works, and that my inner self knows right well.

PSALM 139:13–14 AMPC

When does life begin? The scriptures are clear: from the moment of conception. Here King David declares the wonder and miracle of human life. Every individual of every race, color, and creed is precious to our heavenly Father, knit together within the womb with precision and grace.

Before you were even conceived, God knew you and had a plan for your life. How amazing to think that the Creator and God of the universe charted your life before you were ever formed in your mother's womb.

Vast intelligence involving deliberate thought and complexity is found in the creation of a human being. Even so, the Bible has been questioned and refuted throughout history.

The fact remains: human beings possess intricate features at the anatomical, cellular, and molecular levels. Such intricacies never could have evolved but are the result of intelligent design. Imagine looking at the electrical complexities of, say, your living room lamp. Do you, for one moment, consider that the lamp simply evolved? Not for a second. In fact, to think such a thing is ludicrous. You know for certain that someone constructed it into the lamp you enjoy today. Yet many unbelievers claim that life has evolved over billions of years as they discredit all claims of the magnificent handiwork of our God through His divine creation: you and me.

King David knew better. From the depths of his being he praised God for the magnificence of His handiwork. You, too, are fearfully and wonderfully made in God's own image. So celebrate life.

41. Precious Promises

His divine power has given us everything we need for a godly life through our knowledge of him who called us by his own glory and goodness. Through these he has given us his very great and precious promises, so that through them you may participate in the divine nature, having escaped the corruption in the world caused by evil desires.

2 PETER 1:3–4 NIV

It's all there. Everything. A new identity. Purity and power. Wisdom and strength. Truth and grace. All we need to become like Jesus, He provides.

Some Christians work hard trying to be good. They strive to live up to impossible standards. It's a setup for pride when they do well and debilitating shame when they don't. It's as if they believe Jesus saved them from their past, but when they accepted His gift of salvation they were required to take it from there.

That's not what scripture teaches. Jesus didn't die to save His chosen ones and then leave them on their own to struggle to live a righteous life. He cleanses His people by His blood and then moves inside them in the Person of the Holy Spirit to empower them for all He desires.

God's very nature becomes a part of the believer. God gives His goodness and glory to His children. He covers them with Himself, creating a completely new and pure identity—a new creation—and empowering His people to live in a new way. A way that looks like Jesus.

The Christian's job isn't to strive for perfection but rather to get to know Jesus and receive what He has already given. As we discover who Jesus is and what is important to Him, our perspective changes. We long to be more like the One who loves us. We want to give back to Him and others the love and kindness we experience. He is eager to help us do just that! The Bible says God gives us both the desire and the will to obey Him! Isn't that freeing? From His position within us, God's Spirit changes us. "And the Lord—who is the Spirit—makes us more and more like him as we are changed into his glorious image" (2 Corinthians 3:18 NLT).

Now that is *good* news!

42. Right on Time

The Lord does not delay [as though He were unable to act]
and is not slow about His promise, as some count slowness,
but is [extraordinarily] patient toward you, not wishing
for any to perish but for all to come to repentance.
2 PETER 3:9 AMP

We are an impatient people, especially in this culture of instant gratification. Fast-food restaurants do a booming business. Refrigerators dispense ice and water on demand. Microwaves cook veggies and cereal in a fraction of the time it would take on the stovetop. Computers and the Internet make online purchasing, banking, and bill paying easy and quick. We can keep up with friends with social media, eliminating the need for phone calls or letter writing or even e-mails. Every day new technology comes out making yesterday's phones, computers, and other techy gadgets obsolete almost as soon as they are bought.

So when we are forced to wait on a doctor to see us, on a baby to arrive, in line at the grocery or department store, we express our dissatisfaction, if not in words, in our expressions or body language.

Peter talks about this tendency toward impatience in his second letter to the believers in the first century after Christ's ascension into heaven and the establishment of the church. He quoted unbelievers and believers alike in questioning, "So what's happened to the promise of his Coming? Our ancestors are dead and buried, and everything's going on just as it has from the first day of creation. Nothing's changed" (2 Peter 3:4 MSG).

Peter's answer is similar to Isaiah's answer to the scoffers of his time: God's timing is not ours. We don't have to understand it because He doesn't think or perform as we expect Him to. But because He isn't willing that any should perish and spend eternity without Him, He is patiently waiting. He is never slow to fulfill His promises. His timing is impeccable, spot-on. Always. If He said He will do something, He will. His faithfulness is key to His character and characterizes everything He does.

43. Keep a Firm Grip

*So let's do it—full of belief, confident that we're presentable
inside and out. Let's keep a firm grip on the promises
that keep us going. He always keeps his word.*
HEBREWS 10:22–23 MSG

God is faithful. When He does something, He does it all the
way. No half effort. He is completely trustworthy. Consider His
plan to save His people through Jesus. For centuries sacrifices
were offered to atone for the sins of the people. But God knew
the blood of animals could never save. From the beginning He
had a plan to settle the account once and for all.

Paul explains, "As a priest, Christ made a single sacrifice for
sins, and that was it! . . . It was a perfect sacrifice by a perfect
person to perfect some very imperfect people. By that single
offering, he did everything that needed to be done" (Hebrews
10:11–18 MSG).

God made this plan because He longed for intimacy with
His children. He loves us and has faithfully worked throughout
history to restore us to relationship with Him. God's faithful
work is so complete that believers are now free to draw close to
Him. "So, friends, we can now—without hesitation—walk right
up to God, into 'the Holy Place'" (10:19 MSG).

So let's do it! Let's come with confidence right into the
presence of God, holding on to His faithful promise that our
presence is not only desired but perfectly acceptable! As we walk
out our faith in the everyday world, let's keep a firm grip on *all*
God's promises. If He was faithful to take our imperfect selves and
purify them so we could live forever in His presence, not hesitating
to sacrifice His own Son, won't He be faithful in all things?

Life brings plenty of challenges, and it's easy to forget the extravagant measure God went to on our behalf. But even if we forget, He is faithful to His Word. He cannot lie. Next time you feel your faith slipping, why not take a time-out to ponder His extraordinary and complete commitment to you? Remember how fully He rescued you and changed you, and then keep a firm grip on His promises! "We're not quitters who lose out. Oh, no! We'll stay with it and survive, trusting all the way" (10:39 MSG).

44. Bless Him for His Blessings!

*Bless the LORD, O my soul, and forget not all his benefits, who forgives
all your iniquity, who heals all your diseases, who redeems your life
from the pit, who crowns you with steadfast love and mercy, who
satisfies you with good so that your youth is renewed like the eagle's.*
PSALM 103:2–5 ESV

It's easy to forget God's blessings. God performed mighty
miracles before Pharaoh, freeing His chosen people from slavery
and the tyranny of false gods, yet as soon as they were free
and on their way to the Promised Land, they forgot Him and
complained about their "untenable" situation to Moses. God
performed mighty miracles through the prophet Elijah; yet
days later he prayed for God to take his life in fear of Jezebel's
armies (1 Kings 18–19). We're the same. God repeatedly proves
His mercy and love to us, yet at the first sign of trouble, we get
spiritual amnesia. Rather than praising Him, we trip into the
habit of grumbling and complaining.

Here the psalmist instructs us to bless the Lord and, while
we're at it, remember just what He has done for us. He forgave
our sin; healed our diseases; redeemed our lives from the pit;
continues to extend His love, mercy, and protection toward us;
and gives us only what is good so that our youth is renewed like
the eagle's.

But what does that mean? Naturalists say that when an eagle
turns one hundred years old, she sheds all of her feathers so that
new ones grow back and she is youthful again. Imagine that! Just
as God's blessings are new every morning, our youth, vitality,
strength, substance, health, provision, grace, mercy, and love burst
forth into new life through our relationship with Jesus Christ. He
has promised to bless us if only we will follow Him and His Word.

If you are flailing like a wounded bird in flight, hang on to this verse and claim it as your own. You are God's own, and He won't forsake you. Don't forget what He's done for you in the past; He has even more blessings in store for you ahead, no matter what your circumstances look like now. Begin to bless and praise God.

45. Imperfections Made Perfect

The LORD will perfect that which concerneth me:
thy mercy, O LORD, endureth for ever:
forsake not the works of thine own hands.
PSALM 138:8 KJV

You strive but fall short; you work but fail; you love, but that love is marred with nicks and scratches of unresolved conflicts or unmet expectations. You want to do what's right but often do wrong instead. Why is that? Because we are flawed human beings.

Yet this verse tells us that the Lord will perfect our imperfections. When we come to Christ, we are, as the scriptures teach, new creations. Old things pass away and all things become new. Our journey with Him begins as He changes our hearts, our desires, our outlook, and our very character.

The apostle Paul said he was confident that the One who began a good work in him would complete it (Philippians 1:6). He perfects our imperfections through the power of the Holy Spirit working within us. We are God's workmanship, His masterpiece, made in His image and fashioned by His hand. Nothing we do from the point of salvation onward goes unnoticed by our omnipotent Father.

God uses every trial and adversity to mold you into His image and shape you into the person He planned for you to become from before the beginning of time. God used Moses, a man with a stuttering tongue, to deliver the Israelites from bondage. He used Gideon, "the least in his father's house" by his own admission, to conquer the Midianites. He chose Mary, a young virgin, to become the mother of the Savior. He "perfected" that which concerned all of these saints of old and many more. Likewise, He does the same for you. He takes your weaknesses and turns them into strengths. He "perfects" the imperfect.

46. Never Destitute

*I have been young and now I am old, yet I have not seen
the righteous forsaken or his descendants begging bread.*
PSALM 37:25 NASB

David spoke from the place of experience and knowledge, a life lived. As he stood on the shore of eternity, his observation of the world broadened. He saw it all and he could, with assurance, say that he never witnessed God's people in an impoverished state.

The same is true today. How many times have you heard a story about how God met someone's need just in time? Perhaps they were down to their final meal, their last dollar, and had nowhere to turn. But God came through.

In biblical times, the Israelites were both rich and poor, but none were very poor. The social expectations at that time were to lend to those in need without interest. A year of jubilee—every seven years—was a time when all debts were remitted and mortgaged lands returned to their original owners or their families. Begging was rare if not impossible altogether.

The story of Naomi and Ruth bears out this truth. Showing a distinct lack of trust in God's ability to provide in a time of famine, Naomi and her husband left Bethlehem and moved to Moab with their two young sons. Years later, Naomi returned to her hometown, a widow and childless, with only one of her daughters-in-law with her. Once they were settled, Ruth asked Naomi if she couldn't glean in the fields for the food they so desperately needed. Ruth then "happened" on Boaz's field and stopped to glean behind his reapers (Ruth 2:3). Boaz, a kinsman of Ruth's dead husband, learned who she was, and he made provision for his reapers to leave her more than usual to glean. Later, Boaz married Ruth, providing a home for Naomi at the same time (4:14–15), and she praised God for fulfilling His promise to provide her every need.

Perhaps you are struggling to pay a bill, buy groceries, or fill up your gas tank. If so, begin to cleave to this verse and pray. God won't forsake those who belong to Him. Who knows whom He'll use to bless you, or what circumstances He will orchestrate that will turn things around. You may not have all of your wants met, but He promised to meet every need.

47. He Is with You until the End of the Age

"Go therefore and make disciples of all the nations, baptizing
them in the name of the Father and the Son and the Holy Spirit,
teaching them to observe all that I commanded you; and lo,
I am with you always, even to the end of the age."
MATTHEW 28:19–20 NASB

Most Christians recognize these verses as the Great Commission, the task Jesus laid on all His followers just before He returned to heaven after His resurrection. But it is more than His last spoken command to His disciples. It contains a wonderful promise as well.

As love for our Savior grows, so does our desire to do all He asks of us. Most Bible-believing churches have missionaries they support and pray for regularly. They see it as doing their part of fulfilling the Great Commission. But this command is directed at each of us individually, not necessarily corporately. While the latter is certainly part of it, each of us is to go and do our best to fulfill this command.

Luke, the writer of the book of Acts, also recorded Jesus' last command to His disciples: Go, make disciples, in Jerusalem first. Then Judea, Samaria, and finally to all the world. While God doesn't call all of us into foreign missions, He does expect us all to be witnessing for Him wherever you live, in your "Jerusalem." None of us is excused. But that's where the promise comes in.

Did you see it? Matthew quotes Jesus as saying, "I am with you always." Luke has a little twist to it: "After the Holy Spirit has come upon you." When Jesus ascended into heaven, He promised to send the Holy Spirit to indwell each believer. That happened on the Day of Pentecost; today the Holy Spirit indwells us from the moment we receive salvation in Jesus Christ

alone (1 Corinthians 12:13; Romans 8:9; Ephesians 1:13-14).
God is literally with us wherever we go.

With God indwelling us and going wherever we go, then
fulfilling the command in these two passages is doable. We have
His power and His presence to draw on as we go about daily
living lives that are pleasing to Him. He never gives us a task that
we must complete on our own. He is always with us—guiding,
helping, encouraging.

48. He Will Not Leave You until His Promises Are Fulfilled

*"Behold, I am with you and will keep you wherever you go,
and will bring you back to this land; for I will not leave
you until I have done what I have promised you."*
GENESIS 28:15 NASB

When Rebekah conceived, she soon learned she was carrying twins. The Lord told her two nations would be born from her and their gestation period in her womb was just the beginning of hundreds and thousands of years of strife. He also said the elder would serve the younger.

When the boys were born, Esau came into the world first, lusty and ruddy; Jacob followed, clinging to Esau's heel. As they grew up, each had very different interests in life.

Then Esau sold his birthright to Jacob in exchange for a bowl of stew, he was so hungry. Not long after, Isaac believed he was going to die soon, so he sent Esau out for some wild game for his dinner and told him he would give him the firstborn's blessing when he returned with the food he was craving. Unwilling to wait on God's timing, Jacob and Rebekah plotted to get the blessing for Jacob.

Isaac was deceived and blessed Jacob with all the rights of the firstborn and the covenant promises given to Abraham and Isaac. When Esau returned, he discovered his brother's deception.

Because of Esau's anger, Jacob fled and headed to Rebekah's family. One night the Lord came to Jacob in a dream to reassure him he was Isaac's heir, and the promises of the covenant He'd made with Abraham were his. Then came the promise recorded in Genesis 28:15.

When Jacob woke the next morning, he built an altar to the

Lord before he resumed his journey. Years later, God brought Jacob back to land He had promised to Abraham, Isaac, and Jacob. He now had a large family and much wealth. Rebekah was gone, but Isaac still lived, and Esau had forgotten his anger with maturity and a large family of his own.

God remained with Jacob all the rest of his life. God faithfully fulfilled every promise He gave Jacob that night, and when he returned to his homeland, Bethel was one of the first places Jacob visited in order to give thanks to the Lord for His faithfulness to keep all His promises.

49. Joy in His Presence

You will show me the path of life; in Your presence is fullness of joy;
in Your right hand there are pleasures forevermore.
PSALM 16:11 AMP

Did you ever meet someone who exuded such joy that it filled the room? A joy that has no basis in circumstances or people or emotions. A joy that comes from knowing Jesus Christ and His grace. That's the kind of person everyone wants to be around.

The joy the psalmist refers to in this verse is so much more than any we have or ever will experience on this imperfect earth. And the Person in whom this joy radiates fills not only a room but the entire universe with the brightness of His presence and His unbounded, endless power and love. Paul speaks of this joy in his letter to the Philippians

In God's presence is fullness of joy. Imagine joy multiplied to the extent of total completion and perfect satisfaction. This kind of joy can come only from the creator and giver of joy. On earth, we experience only a measure of happiness, just as God provides us a measure of faith. Yet in our eternal home is "joy unspeakable and full of glory," just as the old hymn declares.

Jesus sits at the right hand of the Father in glory. Throughout the scriptures, the "right hand" denotes a place of highest honor. At the right hand of the Father is Jesus Christ Himself, the author and finisher of our faith and the source of all joy, pleasure, and happiness.

Human happiness is fleeting. We experience moments of happiness and periods of joy, but all are limited. This verse, however, gives us a glimpse of the joy and pleasures to come in our eternal home with Christ. Earthly joy fades, while God's joy is eternal and lasting.

"It is joy unspeakable and full of glory, oh, the half has never yet been told."*

50. What He Promises, He Performs

"God is not a man, so he does not lie. He is not human,
so he does not change his mind. Has he ever spoken and failed
to act? Has he ever promised and not carried it through?"
NUMBERS 23:19 NLT

God can't lie. In fact, it is impossible for Him to do so (Hebrews 6:18). For God to lie is a contradiction of His nature and divine will. His Word and His promises are unchanging, just as God's divine nature never changes. His promises are a result of His eternal purpose that is never altered.

In a courtroom, witnesses may swear on the Bible before they take the stand, giving an oath to "tell the truth, the whole truth, and nothing but the truth." And that settles the matter. To take an oath on God's Word is to pledge to tell the truth on the foundation of all truth, the Holy Scriptures.

Human beings constantly change their minds. What we promise one day, we renege on the next. That's part of human nature. We are imperfect, while God, in His perfection, shows no variableness or shadow of turning (James 1:17).

In this scripture the prophet Balaam reminds Balak, the king of Moab, of this immutable truth: God's promises and decrees are unalterable and sacred. In this context of scripture Balaam informs Balak—who had hired Balaam to curse the children of Israel—that once God blesses, nothing and no one can reverse it. God blessed Israel with His presence, and nothing Balak did to destroy the nation would prevail.

Does unanswered prayer cause you to question God's faithfulness? Do you wonder if you can take God at His Word? Wonder no more. What He promises, He performs. And that's the truth.

God hath not promised skies always blue,
Flower-strewn pathways all our lives through;
God hath not promised sun without rain,
Joy without sorrow, peace without pain.

But God hath promised strength for the day,
Rest for the labor, light for the way,
Grace for the trials, help from above,
Unfailing sympathy, undying love.
ANNIE JOHNSON FLINT

51. He Gives Rest

*"Come to me, all of you who are weary and
carry heavy burdens, and I will give you rest."*
MATTHEW 11:28 NLT

A preacher once said the most spiritual thing he could do was
to sleep eight hours every night. In this passage Jesus is referring
to a different kind of rest. The Pharisees put heavy burdens of
religious living upon the people. The list of rules was extensive
and difficult. Jesus is a different kind of teacher. Instead of
imposing His will, He bears the brunt of the burden and then
walks next to His people every step.

He says, "Let me teach you, because I am humble and gentle
at heart, and you will find rest for your souls. . . . The burden I
give you is light" (Matthew 11:29–30 NLT).

Jesus didn't introduce a new religion to the world; He offers a
relationship with God, one in which He empowers us for all He
asks of us. Whether we are struggling to live right or to hold on
to our faith or to find joy in acts of service, He never asks us to
strive alone. He *always* offers His strong back for our burdens.

Jesus understands we need all kinds of rest. Yes, we need
spiritual rest from the body of sin He came to rescue, but we also
need physical rest and emotional rest. The preacher who talked
about getting sleep has a point. If we push our human bodies too
far, even in service to God, they will grow weary!

Our loving Jesus offers us the unforced rhythms of grace.
They include periods of physical and emotional rest. After long
seasons of trial or service, He often invites us into healing rest.
Sometimes we need weeks or even months away from the battle
to rejuvenate. Resisting the invitation to rest only prolongs the
healing process.

Jesus isn't a taskmaster. He is a loving Lord who cares about those He calls to Himself. *The Message* puts Matthew 11:28 this way: "Are you tired? Worn out? Burned out on religion? Come to me. Get away with me and you'll recover your life. I'll show you how to take a real rest. Walk with me and work with me—watch how I do it. Learn the unforced rhythms of grace. I won't lay anything heavy or ill-fitting on you. Keep company with me and you'll learn to live freely and lightly."

52. The Battle Is the Lord's

*"Do not be afraid! Don't be discouraged by this mighty army,
for the battle is not yours, but God's."*
2 CHRONICLES 20:15 NLT

Life is a battle, and we need a good set of armor to fight it.
Thankfully, the Lord equips every believer with the whole armor
of God to withstand the enemy's attacks (Ephesians 6:13). But
do you ever feel as if your battle is so intense, so continuous, that
no amount of armor or ammo can win it?

Throughout scripture, God instructs His people, "Be not
afraid," or "Be strong and courageous," or "Be not afraid of
them." The reason is clear. God was with them. Despite the bleak
outlook or the multitude of enemies that surrounded God's own,
the Lord would ultimately fight their battles and bring them
through to victory.

That was the case in this portion of scripture. The Moabites
and Ammonites were in hot pursuit against the nation of Judah.
When Jehoshaphat heard that vast armies were headed their way
to destroy the Israelites, he prayed and called a fast. He admitted
to God, "We are powerless before this great multitude who are
coming against us" (2 Chronicles 20:12 NASB).

Have you ever felt that way? Crushed between a virtual rock
and a hard place, you may have felt helpless. You did everything
you knew to do and could do no more. But in this same verse,
the bewildered king confessed, "We do not know what to do, but
our eyes are on you" (NIV). That was the beginning of winning the
war. It placed Jehoshaphat and the Israelites in the background,
and God in the forefront of the battle.

God was, and is, the answer. Man-made swords are defense-
less against the enemy's attacks. The moment we recognize that

the battle we face is not ours, but God's, is the moment we begin to make ground and win.

God told the Israelites they wouldn't have to fight the Moabites and Ammonites. In verse 17 He instructed them simply to praise God and "stand and see the salvation of the LORD" (NASB). They did just that, and their enemies destroyed each other.

Are you in a battle? Hold fast, and with praise on your lips and faith in your heart, remember, this struggle is not yours; the battle is the Lord's.

53. His Sheep Lack Nothing

The LORD is my shepherd, I lack nothing.
PSALM 23:1 NIV

Have you ever been able to say, "I don't need a thing!" If you have, you're one of the few. Yet that's what the psalmist David said in this verse. Although he was a king and undoubtedly enjoyed the perks of that lofty position, he also was human. And humans have needs. So what was his secret?

David wasn't always royal. In fact, the opposite is true. As a young shepherd boy, he understood early on the role and purpose of shepherding. From the beginning, David trusted the Lord. At the time of this writing, David had weathered many a storm and his years of experience taught him that God would come through despite the circumstances. David leaned on the One who had supplied every necessary provision throughout his lifetime.

Through hard times, good times, times of great sorrow, and times of joy, the Lord cared for David as a shepherd cares for his sheep. So with confidence and assurance, the aging king testified that because the Lord was with him—guiding and directing his way—he had no needs.

One of the many names of God is Jehovah-jireh (Yahweh-yireh), meaning "God will provide." The name has its origin in a place in the land of Moriah where God told Abraham to offer his son Isaac as a burnt offering. When the Lord provided a ram for Abraham to sacrifice in place of his son, the ancient patriarch named the place Jehovah-jireh—God the provider (Genesis 22:14).

This verse serves as a constant reminder that because Christ is the Shepherd of our souls, we have everything we need. When finances are slim, God provides. When trouble comes, God makes a way of escape. When illness attacks, God strengthens and heals. Whatever our need, our God provides according to His riches in glory in Christ Jesus. Because of Christ, we have everything we need.

54. Our Healer

O LORD my God, I cried to you for help,
and you restored my health.
PSALM 30:2 NLT

God heals. Moreover, He is the author of all healing. In this verse, David suffered from illness, although the exact form of disease is unknown. Some note that whatever the sickness, it was a dangerous one, so much so that David anticipated death. After fervent prayer, however, God healed him.

Disease and illness are no strangers to us. The ancient saints serve as living illustrations of God's divine intervention. God's Word never changes and is as relevant today as it was thousands of years ago. But does God always heal? Often not in the way we'd like. But He works through every pain and trial to bring forth His divine will in our lives.

Sometimes God heals through effective medical treatment or through a gradual improvement of one's health and well-being. For instance, Terry was diagnosed with a form of dystonia, or movement disorder. The uncontrollable movements caused pain and diminished her quality of life. She received medical treatments that helped, but she still suffered daily. Terry, a devoted Christian, knew her source wasn't medicine alone. She sought the Lord for healing and four years later her doctor was amazed at her vast improvement, which extended beyond what her medical treatment could achieve. "It's near miraculous!" the doctor exclaimed during one of Terry's office visits. Medically, however, Terry still had the disorder. So did God heal her? Terry would say definitely yes.

Sometimes God heals instantly; other times—for reasons unknown to us—He heals gradually over time. Regardless, the

Lord is the author of healing.

Physical healing, however, is only one way God heals, for healing comes in different forms. We need emotional and spiritual healing as well. Do you suffer from anxiety or depression? Are there issues you struggle with or unnecessary burdens you carry? God is your healer.

David sought God, and God healed him. That's the message of this verse. When trouble plagues us, we're moved to pray the kind of prayers that move the very hand of God, our Healer.

55. Delight in Him and Blessings Follow

Delight yourself in the LORD;
and He will give you the desires of your heart.
PSALM 37:4 NASB

What's your greatest source of contentment and joy? From who or what do you derive your happiness? Here the scriptures instruct us to delight ourselves in the Lord. And with that instruction comes a promise: He will give you the desires of your heart.

For many of us, our source of joy varies and our happiness tends to be short-lived. For instance, you purchase a new car and feel elated on the drive home. . .but then you have to make the first payment. Or how about when your baby smiles for the first time? Joy erupts like a marching band heralding the entrance of royalty. But you soon discover that with your precious infant come major responsibilities and sleepless nights, too. Or perhaps you dieted for months to shed ten pounds. One morning, the scale greets you with good news and you're elated! But after consuming a few celebratory desserts, the pounds creep back.

Happiness is fleeting. Rather than deriving joy from earthly events or people, God wants us to get our happiness and contentment from Him. When we do, blessings follow. The term "desires of your heart" comes from the Hebrew word *mishaloth*, meaning requests, petitions. In other words, if we petition the Source of joy for our happiness, well-being, and contentment, He will answer and bless us with "joy unspeakable and full of glory"!

Praise God, from whom all blessings flow;

Praise Him, all creatures here below;
Praise Him above, ye heavenly host;
Praise Father, Son, and Holy Ghost.

56. You Can't Outgive God

"Give, and it will be given to you: good measure, pressed down,
shaken together, and running over will be put into your bosom.
For with the same measure that you use, it will be measured back to you."
LUKE 6:38 NKJV

RG LeTourneau, an inventor and manufacturer of earth-moving equipment, was an amazing man of God. He committed early in life to tithing his income to the Lord, even when his companies failed and left him with enormous debts to pay off. When he told his accountant, sent by the surety company, that he had pledged five thousand dollars to his church's missions fund, the man was flabbergasted and told RG it was the most irresponsible thing he had ever heard for a man carrying one hundred thousand dollars in debt. But that year RG determined to do what he had pledged to his business partner, God, and as he honored the Lord with his finances, the Lord honored him.

Once RG began to manufacture his earth-moving equipment as a full-time business instead of a sideline to his road construction company, he never fell into debt again. Starting his new business (God still was his partner) at the beginning of the Great Depression didn't make sense in human thinking, but in just a few years he paid off his debts and began making money at an astounding rate. Soon he was tithing 90 percent to the Lord, keeping only 10 percent for his own needs. He said, "It's not how much of my money I give to God, but how much of God's money I keep for myself." RG and his wife, Evelyn, started the LeTourneau Foundation to manage the generous donations out of their 90 percent tithe to various Christian organizations and institutions. And God continued to prosper RG until he died in 1969 at the age of eighty-nine.

While not everyone is gifted with the spiritual gift of giving or hospitality, all believers are challenged to be faithful stewards of what the Lord has given them. It doesn't matter what our station in life is—whether we have a lower-, middle-, or upper-class income—when we are obedient to the exhortation Jesus gave His disciples, God promises to give in return much more than we give out: "pressed down, shaken together, and running over."

57. God Supplies All We Need

And my God will liberally supply (fill until full) your
every need according to His riches in glory in Christ Jesus.
PHILIPPIANS 4:19 AMP

All—such a small word, packed with such huge meaning. You may
have heard this quote: "All means all, and that is all, all means."

Within the context of the letter to the Philippians, Paul was
thanking the Philippian church for taking such good care of him
over the years, but he was especially grateful for the last gift they
had sent to him in the prison in Rome. It wasn't so much the
size of the gift as the love and caring behind it. They sent their
gift with one of their own, Epaphroditus. But once he arrived in
Rome and delivered the gift to Paul in prison, Epaphroditus got
sick (see chapter 2). Paul says it was a sickness unto death. Once
Epaphroditus recovered, however, Paul sent him back to Philippi
with the letter he had written, partly in thanks.

Paul's thank-you acknowledged that he knew the people in
the church there weren't wealthy, so they truly had given to him
out of their own need. Because of their generosity, Paul knew
God would supply all their needs according to the riches they
had in Christ Jesus.

In context, most biblical scholars agree that Paul meant the
Lord would provide for all their physical needs, just as He had
healed Epaphroditus so he could return to the church there in
Philippi. But that little word *all* encompasses so much more. It's
not an accident that Paul phrased the sentence in this way.

When we are generous with our time, our money—all the
resources the Lord has blessed us with—He makes sure we are
provided for—physically, spiritually, emotionally, and mentally. In

every way, for every need. All we need to do is ask Him to fulfill His promise. And He will, in His time, from the riches that are stored up for us in Christ Jesus.

58. We Shall Be Like Him

Beloved, now we are children of God, and it has not appeared
as yet what we will be. We know that when He appears,
we will be like Him, because we will see Him just as He is.

1 JOHN 3:2 NASB

You have probably heard it said that the longer a couple is married, the more they resemble each other. The truth of the matter is we become like those we spend time with.

Several times in scripture we read that God's primary purpose for us is to be conformed to the image of His Son, Jesus Christ (Romans 8:28–29). God didn't come up with His plan of salvation just to redeem us from the enemy's hold on us. His plan is so much larger. Part of it includes becoming so like Christ that we reflect Him everywhere we go.

Paul said in Philippians 3 that his one desire was to know Christ, the fellowship of His sufferings and the power of His resurrection. He understood that being conformed to the image of God's Son meant that we must share in His sufferings as well as in His glory. They cannot be separated. But Paul went on to say that he hadn't attained perfection yet. In other words, short of heaven when we finally shed ourselves of the presence of sin in our lives, we cannot fully express all that Jesus is. But John, the longest-living apostle, wrote in his epistle that when Jesus appears to take us home to heaven, then we shall be like Him, for we shall see Him as He truly and perfectly is (1 John 3:2). We will no longer have the old nature and will be able to reflect Jesus perfectly in every aspect.

Paul understood this truth, but it didn't keep him from striving for that goal here on earth. Knowing the promise will be completely fulfilled in heaven, we follow Paul's example and strive to give others a glimpse of our precious Savior in our lives each day.

59. Trust in God and He Will Guide

Trust in the LORD with all your heart, and lean
not on your own understanding; in all your ways
acknowledge Him, and He shall direct your paths.
PROVERBS 3:5–6 NKJV

Has anyone ever said to you, "Trust me! I know this is the right way"? Or "Trust me! Nothing will go wrong"? Yet you know that to trust the person is risky, maybe even dangerous. Still, you have no reason not to trust them in that particular situation. Soon, if you're burned often enough by your friend's "trust me's," you learn not to trust your friend's word on anything.

On the other hand, we all know those who are trustworthy in all they say or do. If they say they will do something, they do it. If they say they know directions to somewhere, they lead you right to the spot. You soon learn to trust them implicitly, and there's never any reason to doubt their word on anything.

God is like that. Because He is omniscient (all-knowing), He knows everything about you. Because He is omnipotent (all-powerful), there is nothing He cannot do, no matter how impossible the task before you seems. Because He is omnipresent, He goes before you into every life circumstance, into every thought, into every motive, into every place you go.

Solomon wrote these words of wisdom to his son: "Trust GOD from the bottom of your heart; don't try to figure out everything on your own" (Proverbs 3:5 MSG). How many times do God's children try to do life on their own, even though they've fallen on their faces over and over again? Like little children who say to a parent or grandparent who wants to help, "No! Do it myself," those who should know better say the same to God: "Leave me alone! I can handle this myself!"

Next time you are tempted to say something similar to God, remember to "listen for GOD's voice in everything you do, everywhere you go" (3:6 MSG). He's the only One who can keep you on track in every situation.

60. He Leads

*Though the Lord gave you adversity for food and suffering for drink,
he will still be with you to teach you. You will see your teacher with your
own eyes. Your own ears will hear him. Right behind you a voice will
say, "This is the way you should go," whether to the right or to the left.*

ISAIAH 30:20–21 NLT

"How can I know God's will for my life?"

People of all ages ask this question.

The simple answer is to listen for His voice. Most often we
hear Him answer through scriptures the Holy Spirit brings to
mind, or through the words of a song, or through advice in a
sermon, a book, or a conversation.

Elijah, after his huge victory over the prophets of Baal, ran
when Queen Jezebel threatened to kill him for his audacious,
God-filled actions. When God "caught up" to Elijah, He asked
him why he was sitting under a juniper tree in the middle of the
wilderness. Elijah answered that his life was done, over. He was
tired of being the only one who cared about serving God. God
could take his life and do them both a favor.

God sent an angel to minister to Elijah, to restore his
strength through food and rest, and then sent him on a journey
to the mountain of God, Mount Horeb. God told Elijah to stand
on the mountain and then sent a very strong wind, strong enough
to break rocks in pieces. But the Lord wasn't in the wind. Then
He sent a strong earthquake, but the Lord wasn't in that either.
Then a fire, but still the Lord wasn't there. Finally He spoke in
a quiet whisper, and Elijah wrapped himself in his mantle and
came out of the cave where he had sheltered to listen.

God said, "I'm not done with you yet." After He outlined
several tasks for Elijah to do, God said, "By the way, you are not

alone in defending Me. There are seven thousand others in Israel who have never bowed the knee to Baal or worshipped him" (see 1 Kings 19).

To know God's will each day, try quieting your spirit to hear His Spirit speak to you, directing every step you take. Turn off your phone. Shut down your computer. Turn off the TV and radio. Sit before God, or better yet, kneel before Him. Ask Him to guide you as He has promised. And listen. He will speak to a heart that truly seeks Him above all else.

61. Our Dwelling Place

He who dwells in the shelter of the Most High
will abide in the shadow of the Almighty.
PSALM 91:1 NASB

"There's no place like home," the familiar saying goes. Home is not only the place where we reside, but a dwelling in which we find solace, rest, and protection from the world. Here the psalmist describes God's presence as a place where we can find protection and comfort in the Lord. We are in Him, and He in us. We reside in the holiest of places, equal to the tabernacle of the Old Testament. Since God inhabits the praises of His people, our most intimate, sacred place is found as we enter into His divine presence through prayer and praise.

The word *shadow* often signifies protection throughout the scriptures, which goes along with the word *shelter*, also indicating a place of protection. In this verse, the picture is that of the outstretched wings of the cherubim, covering the ark and mercy seat. In Exodus 25:20 (NLT), Moses says, "The cherubim will face each other and look down on the atonement cover. With their wings spread above it, they will protect it." It was here that God accepted the high priest's offering once a year on the Day of Atonement, covering the sins of His people and promising to protect them for another year in exchange for their confession of sin.

In essence, the psalmist is saying that those who dwell in Christ enter the Holy of Holies and therefore are covered in the Master's divine protection and care. In all dangers of every kind, we are comforted and shielded under the shadow of the Most High God! Just as a mother shields her baby from the hot sun, or a father removes his child from harm's way, Jesus comforts, protects, and shields us from the heat of life's problems and adversities. He dwells within every believer; likewise, He is our dwelling place.

Welcome home.

62. He Leads through the Darkness

"I will lead the blind by a way they do not know; I will guide them in paths that they do not know. I will make darkness into light before them and rugged places into plains. These things I will do [for them], and I will not leave them abandoned or undone."

ISAIAH 42:16 AMP

"It's like the blind leading the blind," a grandmother said from her place in the passenger seat of the car her young granddaughter was driving.

"What do you mean?" The granddaughter glanced sideways at the old woman. Had she lost her mind? As far as she knew, everyone in the car traveling from Colorado to the tip of Texas could see.

"You're the only one in the car who is old enough to drive who isn't legally blind." Grandma smiled. "Neither your mother nor I can see well enough, but we know the roads the best. And your brother"—she turned to look at him in the middle of the backseat—"thinks he knows all he needs to, but he hasn't a clue, nor is he old enough." She winked at him, effectively silencing his protest.

"So it's like Isaiah said, God is leading this car full of blind and ignorant people. We will get home safely, but only under His watchful care and guidance."

For reasons best known to God, we are driving through life not knowing where we're going or knowing the roads ahead. That's a good thing! If we did know, many of us would turn back in fear and hide from the world and God and never experience the joy and peace He desires to give us as we navigate through the adventures He has for us. Not alone, but with Him. He leads us on paths we don't know. He guides us through the spiritual darkness of this world, shining the light of His Word to illumine the path before us (Psalm 119:105). He smoothes out the rough places and lowers the mountain passes. He does these things for us because He loves us and wants us to experience His best for us. And He never leaves us or abandons us to try to figure out how to escape on our own. What a blessed promise!

63. A Well-Watered Garden

"And the LORD will continually guide you, and satisfy your desire in scorched places, and give strength to your bones; and you will be like a watered garden, and like a spring of water whose waters do not fail."
ISAIAH 58:11 NASB

One of Isaiah's tasks when God called him as a prophet to Israel was not only to prophesy about the coming judgment, but also to comfort God's chosen people as they faced God's justice. But the people wouldn't listen. . .then. Many years passed between Isaiah's words in chapter 58 and the judgment he predicted.

Earlier in this chapter Isaiah records God's unflattering description of His people: "Tell my people what's wrong with their lives, face my family Jacob with their sins! They're busy, busy, busy at worship, and love studying all about me. To all appearances they're a nation of right-living people" (Isaiah 58:1–2 MSG). Outwardly they delighted in going to the Temple and hearing God's Word proclaimed. They rejoiced in their worship, and they were careful to perfectly observe all the laws pertaining to worship. They fasted. They prayed. And they didn't understand why God wouldn't hear their prayers and give them the answers they wanted.

But inwardly and even in public, after they left the Temple they continued to live for themselves, pursuing ungodly pleasures while they fasted. They treated their servants unfairly, to the point of oppression. They fought and quarreled among themselves. God rejected them because of their evil motives. They didn't truly desire to know God, to follow Him with all their hearts, souls, and might (see Deuteronomy 6:4–5), though they declared such a desire daily in their ritual Shema.

God pronounced His judgment on the nation and allowed

Nebuchadnezzar to take His people into exile. It was there God told them that their exile would last seventy years. And He gave them this promise: at the end of their exile, they would truly be His people again. They would carry His Word in their hearts; their motives would be pure. And the Lord would honor their desires and make them like well-watered gardens, like a gushing spring that would never run dry.

Many times believers find themselves in the dry wilderness. They feel they have been in exile, maybe through no fault of their own. But God is ever faithful, and in these times His promises stand true. These dry times don't last forever, no matter what it feels like. The Lord will bring His people out of the wilderness, out of exile, and will make them fruitful—like a well-watered garden, like a gushing spring that never runs dry. What a comfort to know God keeps His promises—always!

64. The Blessings of Obedience

"He will love you and bless you and multiply you;
He will also bless the fruit of your womb
and the fruit of your ground."
DEUTERONOMY 7:13 NASB

What is the single most significant way to show God our love?
Do we give more to His work? Do we work more in and for His
kingdom? Do we make personal sacrifices or strive to become
more like Him? Although all of these things are noble and
noteworthy, we show God our love through a singular act: the act
of obedience.

Not everyone is called to the mission field, but everyone is
called to ministry. How we minister varies as much as human
palm prints. Anytime God has called us to one ministry but we
choose another, disobedience results. Even delayed obedience is
disobedience.

Acts of obedience come in the simplest, smallest forms, such
as holding your tongue when someone unfairly criticizes you, or
listening for God's voice rather than following your own plan.

If we do our part, God will do His. It's that simple. So why
do we make it so complex? In this verse God promises us the
blessings of obedience. If we will love God and follow His moral
and spiritual laws, He not only will bless us but also will bless our
families and everything we possess.

Increase represented blessing in ancient times. Here God
promised that His people would never have heirs without estates
or estates without heirs. If they would keep themselves pure from
the idolatries of Egypt, He would bless them far beyond what
they could comprehend.

Discovering God's will isn't always easy, but if we follow His

Word, then we are following His will no matter where we are in life's journey. When we obey, we demonstrate our devotion to and respect for the Savior. And our obedience reaps rewards. God waits to bless us in innumerable ways. All we need to do is obey.

65. Sleep Safe and Sound

*In peace I will lie down and sleep, for you alone,
Lord, make me dwell in safety.*
Psalm 4:8 niv

Who doesn't yearn for a good night's sleep? The benefits of sleep range from boosting one's mood and improving one's memory to healing one's body and even losing weight! But too many of us lack the knack for getting the sleep our bodies need.

As you lay your head on the pillow, are you able to put to bed your anxieties, worries, and daily pressures? That's often easier said than done. "Get a good night's sleep," we tell the all-star athlete the night before the big game. "Just rest," we coax the patient who is about to undergo surgery. "Get some shut-eye," we say to the overburdened parent. But how can they? How will they?

Bible scholars agree that the phrase "for you alone, Lord" is an expression of absolute confidence. When evil men threatened King David, he claimed Jehovah as his sole protector. Although David wasn't without fear, he knew he could rest safely in God's provisions and promises. He understood that his own wisdom or valor had no effect on his peace of mind or personal security, but rather the only source of tranquility is God.

As we sit at the bedside of a sick loved one, or pore over a mound of bills, or pace the floor waiting for our wayward teen to return home, how can we sleep? If torrential weather or imminent danger threatens our home or life, where do we turn? When the doctor tells us we have an incurable disease or debilitating condition, how do we sleep at night?

Sleepless nights come from carrying unnecessary worries and burdens. Jesus carried our sins and is more than willing and capable to carry our burdens, if we'll let Him. Unbelief and fickleness bring inner turmoil and sleeplessness. But a calm confidence in God yields much-needed rest and sleep. Like a loving parent, the Lord covers us with His divine protection and gives us a soft pillow of peace to rest our harried hearts and minds.

66. Thoughts That Bring Peace: Part 1

*"The steadfast of mind You will keep in
perfect peace, because he trusts in You."*
ISAIAH 26:3 NASB

In Judges 6 we read the story of Gideon. The people of Israel had sinned and found themselves enslaved to the Midianites for seven years. After seven years God heard their cries for deliverance and appeared to Gideon while he was threshing wheat in a winepress. Now, Gideon was a man who was not at peace, with himself or with his captors. He was hiding in a low spot, hoping to get his little amount of wheat threshed without the Midianites finding out and confiscating it. God appeared to him in the form of an angel and told Gideon He wanted him to lead an army of Israelites to free themselves from the Midianites' bondage. Gideon, wanting to be assured this wasn't a dream, asked the Lord to stay there while he went to prepare a meal for Him.

When Gideon returned with the meal, God told him to put the food on a nearby rock and pour the broth over it. Gideon did as he was told, and God honored the sacrifice by consuming it with fire. At the same time Gideon could no longer see the angel of the Lord, and he was terrified. He realized he had truly been talking to God, and he was positive he was going to be struck dead on the spot. But God spoke to him once more and assured Gideon he wouldn't die; God had a plan for him. In gratitude, Gideon built an altar and named it *Jehovah-shalom*, for the incredible peace that flooded him when he believed God's promise.

This story reveals the importance of having a right relationship with God in order to experience peace on a constant basis. Isaiah 26:3 says God will keep us in perfect peace as long as we keep our minds on Him. Peace comes to those who love God's law and keep it (Psalm 119:165). One of Jesus' names is the Prince of Peace (Isaiah 9:6). And Paul tells us in Philippians that we will have peace when we take every one of our cares to Christ in prayer, with thanksgiving, and that peace is a result of right thinking (4:6–9). What a blessed result for those who obey God by giving Him their anxious thoughts and negative thinking!

67. Thoughts That Bring Peace: Part 2

*Fix your thoughts on what is true, and honorable, and right,
and pure, and lovely, and admirable. Think about things that
are excellent and worthy of praise. Keep putting into practice all
you learned and received from me—everything you heard from
me and saw me doing. Then the God of peace will be with you.*
PHILIPPIANS 4:8–9 NLT

In this passage Paul gives us a "test" for our thought life if we
want to have God's perfect peace in our hearts and minds. The
verbs *fix* and *think* in verse 9 are in the present imperative active
tense. That means they are commands to do something now,
continuously, and repeatedly. Just as we are to take our negative
thoughts captive (2 Corinthians 10:5), we are to apply all the
positive things Paul mentions here.

First, we are to think on things that are true. Jesus said the
truth is what sets us free (John 8:32). When we focus on what
is true—the principles of God's Word—whatever is not true
will shrivel and die in the truth's light. Next we are to think on
things that are honorable, whatever invites or attracts us because
of its reliance on the truth. Then we are to think on things that
are right or just, things in conformity with God's rules as set
down in His Word. We also should focus on the purity of Jesus
Christ and of God's Word (Psalm 12:6). Those things that are
lovely, admirable, excellent in quality or virtue, and worthy of
commendation round out the list of things we are to think about.

When we look at this list, who comes to mind? Who is true,
honorable, right, pure, lovely, admirable? Who is excellent and
worthy of praise or commendation? Only Jesus Christ fits this
description perfectly. Only when we fix our thoughts on Him will
we experience "perfect peace" (Isaiah 26:3; Philippians 4:8–9).

This peace is "the peace of God [that peace which reassures the heart, that peace] which transcends all understanding, [that peace which] stands guard over your hearts and your minds in Christ Jesus" (Philippians 4:7 AMP).

68. God's Peace

"Peace I leave with you; my peace I give to you.
Not as the world gives do I give to you. Let not
your hearts be troubled, neither let them be afraid."
JOHN 14:27 ESV

Jesus has just shared the Passover meal with His disciples, initiating the first communion. To them it must have been cryptic, this command to drink His blood and eat His body, but He knows what is coming that night and is preparing His beloved friends.

John 14 begins with Christ's admonition, "Let not your hearts be troubled." He then reminds His disciples of His commitment to them and His unity with the Father. The dreams they had when they chose to follow this Rabbi were shortsighted. Their calling was bigger than they could understand. A troubling time was upon them, but a greater plan was at work.

As Jesus prepares His disciples for His death, He offers them two gifts of comfort—the promise that He will always be with them through the Holy Spirit, who will soon indwell them, and the gift of His peace.

The peace of Jesus is powerful. It isn't transient as the peace of the world is. Won by Christ at the cross, this peace begins by reconciling God's creation back to Him. Is there any greater peace than walking in complete unity with our Creator?

This peace is constant, rooted in the absolute truth that God's will and ways are accomplished. It undergirds the believer with confidence that the all-powerful God is personal, working within and without to bring to pass His plan for our lives. We will have trouble on this earth, but Jesus has overcome the world and its problems.

As we lean upon Christ's first gift, the Holy Spirit, our peace deepens. In fact, as we confront our anxiety and "in everything by prayer and supplication with thanksgiving" offer our concerns to God, "the peace of God, which surpasses all understanding," will guard our hearts and minds in Christ Jesus (Philippians 4:6–7 ESV).

In today's scripture we see our Savior cycling back to His initial admonition: "Let not your hearts be troubled"; then He adds, "Neither let them be afraid." Jesus tenderly calls His followers, then and now, to readjust our thinking. As we navigate the confusing and painful parts of life, our trustworthy, loving Father is working in the bigger picture.

69. God Is Working His Plan

*"Stand at attention while I prepare you for your work.
I'm making you as impregnable as a castle, immovable as
a steel post, solid as a concrete block wall. You're a one-man
defense system against this culture. . . . They'll fight you, but they
won't even scratch you. I'll back you up every inch of the way."*
JEREMIAH 1:18–19 MSG

Jeremiah, a powerful prophet of the Lord, faced a lot of
opposition. He often delivered messages people didn't want to
hear. His ministry spanned forty years, but when God called
him to prophesy, he was not very old. He told God, "Hold it,
Master God! Look at me. I don't know anything. I'm only a boy!"

No matter their age, God's people often feel inadequate for
the task He calls them to. Moses made all kinds of excuses about
why he was ill equipped to lead the Israelites from Egypt. The
prophet Isaiah lamented, "Doom! It's Doomsday! I'm as good
as dead! Every word I've ever spoken is tainted—blasphemous
even!" (Isaiah 6:5 MSG). Talk about feeling unworthy of your
calling!

But into those He calls, God pours what is necessary for
them to walk out their destiny. He doesn't only want His work
done; He also wants His people strong and protected. He
instructs. He empowers. He cleanses. The training season can
be intense. God's servants need to be impregnable as a castle,
immovable as a steel post, solid as a concrete block wall. Pressure
will come upon God's messengers, and so He prepares them for
their work, making them stronger than they thought possible.

God knows how much we can handle and when. He walks
us step-by-step into our future, helping us shed whatever
would be a trap for us as we give ourselves to our life's call. The

shedding hurts sometimes as God confronts our weaknesses and petty perspectives, but each day we are made stronger by His Spirit. Sometimes He allows skirmishes that make us tougher. These experiences aren't fun, but through them we are prepared for the future.

The protection of His people is serious business to God. The New International Version puts Jeremiah 1:18–19 this way: " 'Today I have made you a fortified city, an iron pillar and a bronze wall to stand against the whole land. . . . They will fight against you but will not overcome you, for I am with you and will rescue you,' declares the LORD."

70. God's Plan for Good

"For I know the plans I have for you," says the LORD. "They are plans
for good and not for disaster, to give you a future and a hope."
JEREMIAH 29:11 NLT

Jeremiah prophesied in Jerusalem during the end of the long line
of kings in David's line. Babylon had already taken the king and
the first group of exiles into captivity.

In chapter 29, Jeremiah has a message for those already in
exile. He repeats the reasons they are there and then describes
what the Lord wants them to do while they are there. False
prophets were still trying to say that God wouldn't allow the
exile to last long, but Jeremiah warned the people about listening
to their false words. God indeed intended them to remain in
Babylon seventy long years. Many would die in captivity.

But Jeremiah told them to settle into their new home—
to build houses, plant gardens, eat the fruit of their planting,
continue to get married and have children—in other words, to go
about living just as they did at home in Jerusalem. God, through
Jeremiah, told them to seek the peace of Babylon, to pray for
their captors.

He reminded them that after seventy years they would be
released to go back to Jerusalem. God promised them, "I know
the plans I have for you. Plans for good. Plans for a future and
a hope for the future." Though the people couldn't see ahead
that far, God assured them He still had their good in mind. In
fact, He planned the exile to be good for them, purging them
of the sins of both them and their fathers in refusing to obey
His commands, and giving them a hope that would help them
through the many years in exile.

In the same way God has plans for us today. They are plans

for good. They are plans that give us hope, assuring us that God has a plan for our future. These plans not only will be good for us but also will bring glory to God. What could bring more peace than trusting God's plan for our future?

71. Called and Confident in His Purposes

*And we know that God causes everything to work together
for the good of those who love God and are called according to
his purpose for them. For God knew his people in advance,
and he chose them to become like his Son, so that his Son
would be the firstborn among many brothers and sisters.*
ROMANS 8:28–29 NLT

Many if not most believers tend to quote Romans 8:28 whenever
they are going through a trial. After all, what more comfort could
we ask for than knowing God is working out all the terrible
things that are happening to us and making something good
come from them?

But what if the other people involved are also believers? And
what if they believe God is working things out for good in their
lives? How is that fair? And what exactly did Paul mean when he
wrote that God does this for those who love Him and are called
according to His purpose for them?

A wise woman asked her daughter to consider these questions many years ago when the daughter was seeking justice
against the people responsible for ousting her family out of a
ministry they knew was from the Lord. She not only wanted
vindication from the Lord, but also wanted God's punishment
poured out on these people.

The daughter couldn't get the questions out of her mind until
finally she realized God was asking her to forgive those who
had wronged her and her family. Not that they had ever asked
to be forgiven or even acknowledged they had done anything
for which to be forgiven. However, knowing her attitude was
hindering the Lord from working good out of the situation, she
obeyed and forgave the opposition.

Gradually the Lord gave her grace to forgive completely. But it wasn't until years later that she saw the good—and the purpose—that God intended and worked not only in the people involved but also in the ministry. It was far beyond what she could have imagined at the time.

Once again God had kept His promise to work for His people's good, according to the purpose of molding His children into the image of His Son, for His ultimate glory.

72. The Infilling of God's Spirit

"But you will receive power when the Holy Spirit has come upon you;
and you shall be My witnesses both in Jerusalem, and in all Judea
and Samaria, and even to the remotest parts of the earth."
ACTS 1:8 NASB

In his Gospel, John records many of Jesus' final words to His
disciples before He went to the cross. He had poured three
years of His life into these twelve men, trying to prepare them
for the time when He would leave them permanently after His
resurrection. In John 14, Jesus promises to send them a Comforter,
a Helper, One who would continue to teach them the things the
Father and the Son wanted them to know (14:16–17, 26).

This Comforter would dwell within each of them, teaching
them about the Father, reminding them of the things Jesus had
taught them, and empowering them to live godly, holy lives.

This was the "heart of flesh" Ezekiel spoke about when he
prophesied the new covenant that God would make with His
people. And not only was this new way available to the Jews, but
God opened it up to Gentiles as well—unheard of in the Jewish
culture up to that point in time.

Just before His ascension into heaven, Jesus spoke again of
the Holy Spirit who would come to indwell them. Luke, the
writer of Acts, records Jesus' final command: Be My witnesses
not only in Jerusalem, but also in Judea, Samaria, and the farthest
reaches of the world. He knew they couldn't carry out His
commission in their own wisdom or strength, so He repeated
His promise of the Holy Spirit who would give them not only
the words to speak but also the strength they needed for the
enormous task the Lord had set before them. With His power
they could go out with confidence, knowing the Lord had given

them everything they needed to be successful in completing the work He had given them to do.

This promise wasn't just for Jesus' disciples then; twenty-one centuries later, this promise is also for us.

73. Unashamed of the Gospel

I am not ashamed of the gospel, for it is the power of God for salvation
[from His wrath and punishment] to every one who believes
[in Christ as Savior], to the Jew first and also to the Greek.
ROMANS 1:16 AMP

Why would anyone be ashamed to tell others about something
that works? If you found the cure for cancer, would you be
ashamed to tell others about it? Of course not! If you found an
economical way to live on the moon, would you not let everyone
in on the information? Of course you would! If your child hit a
grand slam home run or scored the winning touchdown in last
week's game, would you be ashamed to brag about it to all your
friends? No! Or if your son or daughter ended the school year
with the highest GPA of the entire student body, especially at a
school known for its high academic standards, would you want
to make sure everyone you know hears about it? Of course you
would!

Then why are we hesitant to share with others the best news
of all? The news that Jesus Christ came to earth, took on the
form of man as a baby, made Himself of no reputation, and lived
among poor people with lowly occupations so He could die the
most ignominious death of the time, taking on Himself the sins
of all who had lived, who were living then, and who would live
after Him, suffering total separation from His holy Father who
cannot look at sin, let alone be in its presence—all this for your
sins; all this so you could be freed from the awful penalty of sin;
all this so you could dwell with Him forever in heaven.

What's to be ashamed of in any of that?

The good news of the Gospel has the power to save the most
callous of sinners. There's the promise. No one is too hard, too

sinful, or too completely indifferent for the power of the Gospel to save them. Who are we to decide whether or not and with whom we will share the Gospel? Jesus came so all people would be given the chance to repent. It's the greatest news ever!

74. My Weakness Showcases His Power

But he said to me, "My grace is sufficient for you, for my power is made perfect in weakness." Therefore I will boast all the more gladly about my weaknesses, so that Christ's power may rest on me.
2 CORINTHIANS 12:9 NIV

It's the Christian paradox. When we are weak, then we are strong. God's power is most mightily displayed in His people when His people are most fully aware of their weakness.

When illness, financial hardship, insecurities—weaknesses—plague us, we feel vulnerable, pressed down, inadequate. The temptation is to hide our struggles and wear a mask of strength, even before our Lord. All the while He waits for us to turn our gaze to Him, to seek His divine power for our frailty.

Paul, the writer of this passage, learned a different way. He saw weakness as the place where God shows off, demonstrating how *His* power and *His* grace are the key to powerful living.

Admitting our weakness allows us to let go of self-sufficiency and pride so we can seek—and receive—the endless supplies of God's divine grace and strength for our every need. We don't need to dig deeper and gut it out. We need to step from a place of striving to hide and overcome our weakness to a place of resting in God to work through and in spite of our weakness.

Scripture is clear that God gives His strength to the humble but opposes proud, haughty living. We get off track when we try to bring God glory by showing everyone how strong we are in trial or by hiding behind a mask of sufficiency. Sometimes we dishonor His reputation by our very efforts to protect it. How much more powerful our witness when others see the struggle, how we lean upon our Savior through it all, and how faithfully He carries us.

When we lean into Jesus, laid bare in our insufficiency and believing in His, that's when the world sees the caring, constant, all-powerful God. The Lord told Paul, "My grace is sufficient for you, for my power is made perfect in weakness."

He says the same to us today: Come to Me. I am all you need. My grace shines most brightly in your weakness.

75. Prayers Heard

The LORD is far from the wicked,
but He hears the prayer of the righteous.
PROVERBS 15:29 NASB

"Why bother with praying? God never answers. I'm not sure He even cares."

"My prayers bounce off the ceiling. They never go any higher. At least that's how it feels. God doesn't listen to me."

"Me? Pray? Ha! Why bother? God never hears my prayers. I can do without His help, anyway."

Have you ever heard these statements? Or said them yourself? God truly delights in hearing from His children. But His Word tells us there are several reasons He doesn't hear our prayers.

The primary reason is here in Proverbs 15. God is far from the wicked. Sin puts a barrier between God and us, before *and* after salvation. The only prayer of the unrighteous person God hears is the prayer of repentance and the humble request for salvation. But even the believer, the righteous person, can find his or her prayers blocked. Those prayers do feel like they go no farther than the ceiling.

But sometimes even when we know we are harboring no sin that could prevent our prayers from reaching Him, we still feel as though God is ignoring us. Some believe God doesn't hear unless we pray a certain way, for example, using the ACTS format—adoration, confession, thanksgiving, supplication—or another "formula" type prayer. Some believe that if we don't take time to acknowledge who He is and give Him glory, He doesn't listen. Not true!

Prayers of desperation, He hears and answers. He hears our "popcorn" prayers, short statements of prayer—one form that is effective in corporate prayer. Also, Paul encourages us to "never stop praying" (1 Thessalonians 5:17 NLT), to be constantly in an attitude of prayer. If we are, then some of the formula type prayers are unneeded.

One other reason we believe we don't get answers to prayer could be that we don't get the answer exactly the way we envisioned it, so we don't consider it heard or answered. Also, we may need to wait awhile longer before getting an answer. Yes, no, wait awhile. Just keep the lines of communication free from sin.

76. The Holy Spirit Prays for Us

*The Holy Spirit helps us in our weakness. For example,
we don't know what God wants us to pray for. But the Holy Spirit
prays for us with groanings that cannot be expressed in words.
And the Father who knows all hearts knows what the Spirit is saying,
for the Spirit pleads for us believers in harmony with God's own will.*
ROMANS 8:26–27 NLT

Some Christians put pressure on themselves when it comes to prayer. They worry about saying the right words or using the right method. They burn themselves out with prayer lists or fear God won't hear if they don't have enough faith. They study books and scour scripture for the perfect approach.

God never made it that hard. He delights in our desire to grow in our communion with Him and doesn't mind that we seek instruction. But He is not a God of formulas. He hears no matter how we come to Him.

God says when we don't know what to pray or how to pray, it's okay. The Spirit Himself intercedes on our behalf, connecting our heart to the Father's heart, bringing us into harmony with what God wants us to do.

In times of deep pain or fear, we may have trouble formulating coherent thoughts. But we don't need to worry that we're letting God, ourselves, or loved ones down because our prayers are not eloquent and spilling forth. The Holy Spirit is eager to pray for us in these times. *The Message* says, "If we don't know how or what to pray, it doesn't matter. He does our praying in and for us, making prayer out of our wordless sighs, our aching groans" (Romans 8:26–27).

We often aren't sure *what* to pray. The Spirit knows us better than we know ourselves. He also knows God's plan. He is right there with us. Sometimes He shows us God's will and empowers us to pray it. Other times He simply prays on our behalf.

Prayer is a gift. It's a conversation with Daddy God. A lovers' meeting with Bridegroom Jesus. A teaching session with our guide, the Holy Spirit. But it's not about perfection. Whether we know what to say or sit in silence, the Holy Spirit is always there, connecting us to the Trinity, praying the Father's will.

77. He's Listening

"It shall also come to pass that before they call, I will answer; and while they are still speaking, I will hear."
ISAIAH 65:24 AMP

From the beginning of Daniel's sojourn in Babylon, he was known as a man of prayer. In fact, he determined early on not to let himself become defiled by the wickedness that surrounded him daily. First with what he ate, later in his daily behavior and habits. Prayer set him apart from the others in the kingdom.

So much so that when Daniel was an older man and King Darius made him the head of all the princes and counselors of the kingdom, his enemies knew exactly what to do to topple him from his much-coveted position. They got the king to sign a proclamation that anyone who prayed to anyone other than the king (appealing to his vanity) for the next thirty days would be thrown into the den of lions. No one had ever survived that particular punishment. But even after the proclamation was signed into law, Daniel continued to pray three times a day. Not privately where no one knew, but publicly as he was used to doing—in front of the windows in his chamber that faced toward Jerusalem, he kneeled and openly prayed to God. His enemies immediately told the king, and Darius, grieving that he'd so easily fallen for their plot, had to follow through. So Daniel was arrested, thrown into the den of lions, and left overnight. Darius couldn't sleep that night, but as soon as dawn began to break, he headed back to the lions' den, hoping against hope that Daniel had survived the night. And he had. God had sent an angel to shut the lions' mouths.

Later we read that Daniel had a vision and asked God to reveal the meaning. For three weeks he prayed, fasting and mourning because he received no answer. Finally Gabriel, an angel sent from God, came to him and gave him the understanding he had asked for. He told Daniel that from the first day God had heard his prayer and had sent Gabriel with the answer, but he had been hindered from getting to Daniel for three weeks. Satan had prevented him, and only when the archangel Michael came to help him did Gabriel get away to Daniel.

God does hear our prayers when we first call. And He answers, many times even before we pray! But sometimes the enemy attempts to turn God's answer aside. Persevere. God hears and He answers.

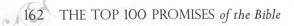

78. When Two Agree

"Again I say to you, that if two of you agree on earth about
anything that they may ask, it shall be done for them by
My Father who is in heaven. For where two or three have
gathered together in My name, I am there in their midst."
MATTHEW 18:19–20 NASB

Throughout His earthly ministry, Jesus taught His disciples the
importance of prayer and gave them instruction on how to pray.
In the so-called Lord's Prayer, He taught them the importance
of taking time to worship God in prayer, even before making our
requests. Often our prayers leave out the aspect of worship and
thanksgiving and focus only on what we want from Him.

But it wasn't just individual prayers that Jesus encouraged; He
also taught the disciples the importance of corporate prayer. Too
often we forget that. The midweek service in many churches used
to be a prayer service—a time when church members met to pray
together over the needs of the local church body. But in the era of
megachurches and busy lifestyles, many churches have dropped
the midweek service. Many have prayer "hotlines" or e-mail lists
that effectively get the word out to pray for certain needs. But
fewer and fewer believers are involved in corporate prayer.

Jesus said when even just two people agree with each other
about anything they pray about, they can expect the Lord to
answer. He went on to say that anywhere two or three people
gather together to pray in His name, He is there listening to
their requests, glorying in their worship, and delighting to answer
their petitions.

One group of women gets together twice a month to pray,
seek the Lord's answers, and intercede on each other's behalf
for their ministries and families. They are from all different

churches and walks of life, but the Lord brought them together over a shared interest and has kept them together to provide encouragement and strength to each other. Jesus is very much a part of their prayer times, and they have seen some amazing answers to prayers as a result.

If your church doesn't have a corporate prayer time, gather a few friends who desire this type of prayer, find a time to meet, and pray. God will honor your time of prayer when you pray in Jesus' name.

You are my hiding place; You preserve me from trouble;
You surround me with songs of deliverance.
PSALM 32:7 NASB

On February 28, 1944, the German Gestapo invaded the home
of Corrie ten Boom's family in search of much-sought-after
Jews. Corrie's father, Casper, her sister, Betsie, and other family
members were arrested and imprisoned.

Meanwhile, for forty-seven hours, six Jewish people hid
behind a false wall constructed in Corrie's bedroom. There, in the
dark, cramped quarters, void of provisions or water, they silently
waited until it was safe to emerge. The Nazi terrorists never
found them, and they all survived.

The ten Boom family and their friends saved an estimated
eight hundred Jews and Dutch underground workers, providing
them with a safe harbor, a hiding place from the Nazis. They
sacrificed their lives for the lives of others. Casper ten Boom,
Corrie's father, died ten days after his imprisonment in
Scheveningen. Corrie and her sister, Betsie, spent ten months
in three different prisons, and Betsie died in Ravensbruck
concentration camp just days before Corrie's miraculous release.
Due to a clerical error, Corrie was freed one week before all the
women her age were executed.

When trials come, where do you go to escape? Have you ever
just wanted to run and hide? We all have. Though we may not
need to flee for our lives, we often require a personal hiding place.
Jesus shed His blood so that we might live. With love, mercy,
and great sacrifice, Christ constructed a wall of protection and
security for every believer.

The Hebrew word for "hiding place" in this verse is *mictar*, meaning "secret place for protection." This verse promises God's protection and safety from the onslaughts of life and from the constant attacks of the enemy of our souls.

Corrie was often quoted as saying, "There is no pit so deep that God's love is not deeper still." No matter how deep your problem, our loving God is your hiding place. So hold on and hide in Christ, because deliverance is on its way.

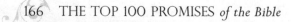

80. A Present Help

God is our refuge and strength,
an ever-present help in trouble.
PSALM 46:1 NIV

Have you ever used OnStar? The service provides immediate assistance should you have an auto accident or a flat tire or need directions. "How may I help you?" the voice asks at the press of a button. Pretty nice. Immediate assistance is what we'd all like but seldom get in today's world.

For example: You phone a doctor's office and go through several prompts before talking to a real person. Then the real-person receptionist transfers the call to a nurse, but the nurse is busy with patients so your call is forwarded to voicemail. Or you have questions about your insurance. You phone the company, and the person on the other end transfers you to another depart-ment, but that person can't help you either, and transfers you to yet another division. You explain your questions to person after person, but no one seems to know the answer. You need help, but help is missing. Big time.

In this verse "an ever-present help in trouble" (NIV) means just that. In fact, the word *present* means "has been found," or He has "proved" himself to be a help in trouble. The word *present* indicates God's closeness to us during these times, and the verbiage used in this text indicates He not only is nearby to help but is *exceedingly* near. What's more, His track record to assist us is impeccable!

God is the Radiant Star who outshines OnStar or any other earthly service that claims to assist us in our most vulnerable, difficult moments. Need help? God is on the scene, even before you realize it. He promises, "I will answer them before they even call to me. While they are still talking about their needs, I will go ahead and answer their prayers!" (Isaiah 65:24 NLT).

81. God's Secret Agents

He will order his angels to protect you wherever you go.
They will hold you up with their hands so you won't even
hurt your foot on a stone.
PSALM 91:11–12 NLT

An oncoming car misses you by inches. Seemingly, an unseen hand removed you from harm's way. Late work nights and too many responsibilities tax your strength. You need a break, but another unexpected problem arises that you must tackle. How do you muster the strength? After prayer, you sense a renewed ability to go on. As you work, you feel as if angels are upholding you on each side.

Contrary to secular stereotypical images, angels are not chubby-cheeked cherubs or mythological creatures born out of a fairy tale. Rather, they are powerful celestial beings created for God's specific purposes.

The scriptures say the Lord sends angels to assist God's own (Hebrews 1:14). Our heavenly Father dispatches these glorious creatures to watch over every detail of our lives and to guard us in all our ways. At God's command they delivered the apostle Peter from prison, shut the mouths of lions, provided needed provisions for Elijah, delivered an amazing message to Mary, and heralded the Savior's birth.

But Satan also used these verses to try to tempt Jesus to sin.

> *Then the devil took him to the holy city, Jerusalem, to the highest point of the Temple, and said, "If you are the Son of God, jump off! For the Scriptures say, 'He will order his angels to protect you. And they will hold you up with their hands so you won't even hurt*

your foot on a stone.'"

Jesus responded, "The Scriptures also say, 'You must not test the LORD your God.'" (Matthew 4:5–7 NLT)

These divine messengers are present and active in our lives today as well. In Psalm 91:11–12, God promises that He will dispatch His angels whenever we have need of them. These "guardian" angels are God's active agents on assignment. They are present at our birth and will carry us to the Father's arms when we pass into eternity. They are God's real secret agents of mercy, strength, and protection.

82. Nothing Can Harm God's Own

"But no weapon that is formed against you shall prosper, and every
tongue that shall rise against you in judgment you shall show to be
in the wrong. This. . .is the heritage of the servants of the Lord."
ISAIAH 54:17 AMPC

Throughout Israel's history, from the time of Abraham until
now, the Jewish people have seen this promise fulfilled over
and over again. While at times their enemies have seemed to
have prevailed, they have never done so for long. The people of
Israel have suffered much hardship over the centuries, some of
it brought on by their own refusal to worship God or obey His
commands to them.

First, God used Moses to free His people from Pharaoh's
slavery. Later He used ordinary people from within Israel to
deliver them from oppressive tyrants. Deborah, Gideon, and
Samson come to mind. Then Israel demanded a king like the
other nations, rejecting the theocracy of God.

When God set Saul in place, the people breathed easier,
thinking their troubles from outside kingdoms were over. Not so.
Saul didn't obey God completely in destroying the Amalekites,
and much later, when the Jews were in exile in Persia, a descen-
dant of the Amalekites tried to annihilate them. God put Esther
in place as queen with influence over the king to thwart Haman's
evil plans.

The list goes on and on through the centuries, but this
passage in Isaiah predicts what would happen after the exile
in Babylon. . .and far into the future to cover believers, both
Jews and Gentiles. Today, the Jews are back in their own land,
though they are still up against their ancient enemies. Even their
Gentile allies (mostly those who don't believe in Jesus Christ) are

deserting them once again.

However, the promise still holds. "No weapon that is formed against you shall prosper." This is our heritage, too. Satan may oppose us, especially when we are doing things that have eternal value, but he is a defeated foe (see Colossians 2), and while it may look as though he is winning, ultimately God wins. His people are vindicated for all eternity.

The next time your back is against the wall, remember nothing will be able to topple you off the firm foundation on which God has put His beloved.

83. Jesus, Our High Tower

The LORD also will be a refuge and a high tower for the oppressed, a refuge and a stronghold in times of trouble (high cost, destitution, and desperation).
PSALM 9:9 AMPC

If you have ever felt crushed, broken, afflicted, or helpless, then you know what it is to experience oppression. This verse assures us that during times of oppression, God is our refuge and high tower. But what does that really mean?

In biblical days, to prevent gnats from biting them, the Egyptians would sleep in high towers where the pesky insects couldn't reach them due to their limited flight abilities. In fact, the Hebrew word for "high place" is *misgab*, indicating the proper height and altitude that would be inaccessible to the enemy. In days of old, the misgab was a place people sought in times of danger to find security and protection. It was a place of safety and retreat.

The Messiah is our divine Misgab. He is the only One in whom we can find peace and refuge during our most difficult moments. Desperation is diminished in His presence; problems lessen and perspectives change when we come to Him in prayer and praise. Too often, though, God seems silent and we feel as if He has abandoned us as the waves of oppression hit with brutal force. But God's timing is perfect.

At the end of this verse, the Hebrew word *batsarah* occurs. Some interpret *batsarah* as meaning defense, but in this context it is rendered "trouble," denoting such adverse circumstances that a person feels there is no way of escape. When we feel completely helpless, we tend to turn to the Lord. So God may allow us to come to the end of ourselves, in utter desperation, so that we depend on Him alone.

He *is* our high tower and refuge in the midst of oppression and distress. When we run to Him, we are safe from the enemy of our souls. As we enter into His high tower, fashioned and built for us, we find relief and peace, and the pests of oppression can no longer reach us.

84. God's Promises Preserve Us

The LORD's promises are pure, like silver refined in a furnace,
purified seven times over. Therefore, LORD, we know you will protect
the oppressed, preserving them forever from this lying generation.
PSALM 12:6–7 NLT

The purest of silver or gold or any other precious metal doesn't
come out of the mines in pristine condition. It is mixed in with
other minerals. It takes people skilled in detecting the ore to
recognize its worth and mine it. And then it must pass through
a rigorous purification process before it is ready for molding into
jewelry or other useful or decorative pieces.

"The silver used by the ancients was probably obtained by
smelting lead sulfide ore, rich in silver (argentiferous galena).
After the ore had been reduced to a metallic condition, the lead
was separated from the silver by blowing hot air over the surface
of the melted metal. The lead was thus changed to lead oxide
which, in a powdered condition, was driven away by the air blast."*

The prophet Ezekiel compared the Israelites to silver going
through a refining process as they went into exile. "The people of
Israel are the worthless slag that remains after silver is smelted.
They are the dross that is left over—a useless mixture of copper,
tin, iron, and lead. . . . 'This is what the Sovereign LORD says:
Because you are all worthless slag, I will bring you to my crucible
in Jerusalem. Just as silver, copper, iron, lead, and tin are melted
down in a furnace, I will melt you down in the heat of my fury. I
will gather you together and blow the fire of my anger upon you,
and you will melt like silver in fierce heat. Then you will know
that I, the LORD, have poured out my fury on you'" (Ezekiel
22:18–22 NLT).

God says His promises are like silver that has been through

the refining process: they are tried, tested, and pure. And we can be sure that if God has promised something, not only is it able to protect and preserve us, but it can never be broken. For God's Word, like God, is eternal truth, and it preserves us forever and ever, just as Israel was preserved as God's chosen people through the refining fires.

---

*"Refiner," Bible Hub, http://biblehub.com/topical/r/refiner.htm.

85. In Our Brokenness

The LORD is near to the brokenhearted
and saves those who are crushed in spirit.
PSALM 34:18 NASB

A mom grieves over her wayward child, a man breaks under the pressures of his job, a woman crumbles after the passing of a loved one, a person suffers with a chronic illness.

What causes a person to break? Prolonged stress or a series of disappointments? Failure or financial pressures? The weight of too much responsibility for too long? Personal loss? The reasons are endless. But here God promises that when you are heartbroken, crushed under the heaviness of affliction or sorrow, God is near. If your world seemingly falls apart, He is present to comfort, encourage, and heal.

In a broken state we might feel vulnerable, but that's the time when God can work in and with us the most. When we feel helpless, we are more apt to seek God for answers. During those moments, our shortcomings are more pronounced, so we see our need for the Lord—for His forgiveness, wisdom, and direction— more than ever before. We've fallen so low that the only place to look is up. And we see God. When we grieve, we have need of the Comforter. Though others might try to help, no one can help us like Jesus.

David, the author of Psalm 34, understood feeling helpless. When he wrote this psalm he was running from Saul, who in his jealous rage had repeatedly tried to kill him. David fled to the Philistine king in Gath, Achish, who was glad to welcome him as an ally against Saul. However, Achish's servants reminded their king that David was a mighty warrior fully committed to God's cause and praised by the people. David feared for his life, and "he pretended to go crazy, pounding his head on the city gate and foaming at the mouth, spit dripping from his beard" (1 Samuel 21:13 MSG). And God delivered him from another potentially dangerous situation.

That's the essence of this verse in Psalm 34. As David was beginning to learn, trials bring humility, patience, and often a much-needed fresh outlook. Through your trials and brokenness comes sweet relief. When you're at your most vulnerable, God is there to heal and help you. He promises to stand alongside you in your darkest hour. Even when you don't sense His presence, rest assured. . .He's near.

86. He Gave His Son

*"For God so loved the world, that He gave His only begotten Son,
that whoever believes in Him shall not perish, but have eternal life."*
JOHN 3:16 NASB

The promise contained in this one verse is probably the best
known in the entire Bible. Jesus spoke it first to Nicodemus, a
Pharisee, a member of the ruling body in Judea, the Sanhedrin.
Nicodemus recognized there was something different about
Jesus, but because of his position, he didn't want to be seen with
Him. So John tells us earlier in the chapter that Nicodemus
came to see Jesus at night. He had a lot of questions about what
it meant to be "born again." And Jesus patiently answered his
questions, including "How can these things be?" (John 3:9 NASB).

First, this verse speaks of the scope of God's love. He "*so*
loved the world." The adverb *so* is often misused today, but it
expresses the ultimate extent in its descriptive role. God loved
the world so much that He was willing to come up with a plan to
save people from themselves.

God created a perfect world and put Adam and Eve into it
with a nature like His own. But they fell when Satan tempted
Eve and sin entered the world, breaking their perfect fellowship
with God. God in His omniscience knew His perfect world
would be marred and prepared a plan to restore that fellowship
even before He laid the foundation of the world (Ephesians 1).

Second, God provided the perfect sacrifice to satisfy His need
for a holy people intent on worshipping Him. "God so loved the
world, that He gave His only begotten Son." His plan called for
His perfect Son to die on the cross, bearing our sin—past, present,
future—as the only perfect sacrifice, the only payment, the only
way to reestablish fellowship with a perfect, holy God.

Last, God's love motivates Him to give eternal life to anyone who believes in Christ's perfect payment for our redemption. They will never perish but will live eternally in heaven with God. The fellowship God desires with His creation has been restored. What a glorious promise! What wondrous love!

87. No Other Way

Jesus told him, "I am the way, the truth, and the life.
No one can come to the Father except through me."
JOHN 14:6 NLT

What an amazingly bold statement Jesus made! It certainly is
one of the most disputed over the centuries since He made it.

How could a loving God make a statement like this? A
loving God would want everyone to be with Him forever, right?
Wrong.

"Oh, it doesn't really matter what you believe or don't believe.
We're all going to end up in the same place. But there are many
ways to get there. All paths lead to the same end."

Maybe you've heard someone say this. At first it sounds good.
After all, why would a loving God exclude anyone from heaven?
But that's not what Jesus taught at all. During His Sermon on
the Mount, He spoke of two paths through life: "Enter through
the narrow gate; for the gate is wide and the way is broad that
leads to destruction, and there are many who enter through it.
For the gate is small and the way is narrow that leads to life, and
there are few who find it" (Matthew 7:13–14 NASB).

In His final discourse to His disciples the night He was
arrested, Jesus answered Thomas's question—"How can we know
the way to where You're going?"—with this simple statement:
"I am the way, the truth, and the life. No one can come to the
Father except through me."

There is only one way. Through Jesus. Through His shed
blood.

The writer of Hebrews said, "We have confidence to enter
the holy place by the blood of Jesus, by a new and living way
which He inaugurated for us through the veil, that is, His flesh"

(10:19–20 NASB). When Jesus talked about the broad and narrow ways, He said the broad way led to destruction, meaning eternal life in hell. The narrow way leads to God, to eternal life in heaven.

We can come to God only through the cross of Jesus Christ. There is truly only one way.

88. No Condemnation

So now there is no condemnation for
those who belong to Christ Jesus.
ROMANS 8:1 NLT

An insidious voice whispers nasty words into the believer's ear:
Unworthy. Guilty. Not good enough. Undeserving. It says, "You
should be ashamed. You'll never live up."

The voice tears down. Shakes up. Destroys.

Even with its evil tone, Christ followers sometimes mistake
it for the voice of conviction. If they just try harder, maybe they
won't feel like such failures. What can they do to live free of
condemnation?

But the snarling voice is not the voice of truth. Scripture
points a clear finger toward the one who is the accuser: Satan
himself (Job 2:1; Revelation 12:10). It is he who comes like
a roaring lion. It is he who kills and destroys. He is the great
deceiver, the father of lies.

The voice of Truth is very different. He comes in goodness.
He says there is no condemnation for those who are saved by
Christ. He declares the blood of Jesus has covered the believer,
cleansing her and making her worthy. He says the believer is a
new creation, a part of the royal family with all the rights and
privileges belonging to a child of God.

Those who long to live a holy life can find it difficult
to discern between the voice of conviction and the voice of
condemnation. It is wise to stop and ponder the tone of the voice
and the resulting fruit of its message.

Accusing, hurtful, condemning thoughts are *never* from the
one who set us free from the darkness. Words that result in guilt,
shame, and hopelessness are to be rejected, not embraced.

Of course the believer is constantly growing and changing, becoming more like Christ. As the Holy Spirit brings about change, He reminds the believer of the victory already won at the cross. With *His* conviction come empowerment, hope, and strength! His personality is full of love, joy, peace, patience, kindness, goodness, faithfulness, gentleness, and self-control, and the tone of His coming reflects the beauty of His character. The One with a voice of Truth is a helper, an encourager, an advocate. He comes alongside the believer, reminding him of who he is in Christ. He cheers the believer on, strengthening him through struggle and establishing him in righteousness.

For the believer, covered with the precious blood of Jesus, there is *no* condemnation. Only love.

89. New Creations!

Therefore if anyone is in Christ, he is a new creature;
the old things passed away; behold, new things have come.
2 CORINTHIANS 5:17 NASB

The scent of a new book. A new bud on a rosebush. The soft cheeks of a newborn. New is special. Not just different, but completely fresh.

Thanks to Christ's work on the cross, Christians not only are different than before; they are *new!* An old car looks better with a new paint job, but the car itself is not new. Christians aren't just given face-lifts, they are remade completely.

In 2 Corinthians 5:21 Paul writes, "He made Him who knew no sin to be sin on our behalf, so that we might become the righteousness of God in Him" (NASB). It's a clear explanation of what it means to be a new creation. Christians trade in their old, sinful, human model for the very righteousness of God Himself.

We are *new.*

Fresh. Pure. Holy. Beautiful.

We don't only think and act differently. We *are* different. Changed-inside-out-through-and-through-completely-remade different.

Ezekiel prophesied about new creations. Through him God promised, "I will give you a new heart and put a new spirit within you; and I will remove the heart of stone from your flesh and give you a heart of flesh" (36:26 NASB).

The Christian's very core is new. Re-created with God's Spirit, it is now tender to the ways of the Lord.

Scripture says we were dead in sin, living in the kingdom of darkness, but Jesus' work raised us from death to life. We moved from the old kingdom into His new kingdom of light.

The old self passed away.

The new self, fashioned by the Spirit of God, is resurrected. This self has old habits but new desires. The Christian learns to pause and connect with God's Spirit within so the old habits pass away and the believer is transformed consistently to behave more and more like Jesus.

The enemy of light tries to convince new believers they haven't really changed, pointing out their mistakes and where they fall short. But his words are simply lies from the depths of darkness.

Hebrews 10:14 puts it this way: "For by the one offering He has perfected forever and completely cleansed those who are being sanctified [bringing each believer to spiritual completion and maturity]" (AMP).

Jesus' death and resurrection changed *everything*. We are new.

90. God's Word Accomplishes His Purposes

"The rain and snow come down from the heavens and stay on the ground to water the earth. They cause the grain to grow, producing seed for the farmer and bread for the hungry. It is the same with my word. I send it out, and it always produces fruit. It will accomplish all I want it to, and it will prosper everywhere I send it."
ISAIAH 55:10–11 NLT

Many of us have either grown up on a farm or know those who farm. Some of us have a farm tradition in our backgrounds. But even if you're an "urban" farmer (that is, a gardener, either vegetable or flower), we can all understand the many farming metaphors and stories found in the Bible.

This passage is a favorite, maybe because we can also see the water cycle we learned about years ago in school: Water in some form (rain, snow, sleet, hail) comes to earth from clouds. It soaks into the ground, eventually making its way into small underground streams that move aboveground and then travel into larger streams and rivers, eventually dumping into the various oceans and seas. The sun evaporates the water, returning it to the heavens. . .and the cycle begins again.

For the purpose of this illustration, though, the water soaks into the ground and waters the seeds the farmer or gardener has planted. As the plants grow and mature, they provide food for all and seeds for the farmers to plant the next season.

God says this example from farming illustrates the way the Word works in people's lives. We plant the seed of His Word deep in our hearts through memorization and meditation. God is the farmer who tends the seed, watching it grow into mature fruit. And it always produces fruit. Always.

The King James Version says God's Word never returns to Him "void." It's an old word that means "empty." In other words, God never sends out His Word without it accomplishing the purpose for which He sent it. Rather, it always, always produces fruit that has eternal value.

91. Following God's Word Leads to Success

"This book of the law shall not depart from your mouth, but you
shall meditate on it day and night, so that you may be careful to do
according to all that is written in it; for then you will make your
way prosperous, and then you will have success."
JOSHUA 1:8 NASB

Before Joshua entered the Promised Land as the new leader of the children of Israel, God came to him and spoke encouragement into his heart. Moses had just finished with his summary of all the Lord had done since delivering them from slavery in Egypt. He included the giving of the law and repeated the high points of that. At the end, Moses said his final farewell. He wasn't allowed into the Promised Land, and he knew he was about to die. Between the end of Deuteronomy and the first chapter of Joshua, God's words to Joshua were meant to encourage him in the task before him.

Merriam-Webster's Collegiate Dictionary defines *success* as a "favorable or desired outcome; also: the attainment of wealth, favor, or eminence." This is how the world views success: how wealthy you are, what kind of favor you have with others, and how eminent your professional or social position is. In the Bible *success* comes from the Hebrew word *sakhal*. In Spiros Zodhiates's *The Complete Word Study: Old Testament*, the author defines this word as "to be circumspect, be prudent; to act prudently; to have wisdom, skill, or expertise; be intelligent, have insight; to be successful (i.e., to act in a prosperous manner)."

To Joshua God defined success this way: to pay attention to and not neglect the Word of God, His law, thereby gaining God's insight on life. Not only was Joshua to read God's Word often; he was to meditate on it and then obey it. Not exactly what success looks like to the world, but which would you rather have—success in the world or success with God? This promise is clearly for those who desire success with God.

92. God's Promises Give Life

I have stored up your word in my heart, that I might not sin against you. . . . This is my comfort in my affliction, that your promise gives me life. . . . I will never forget your precepts, for by them you have given me life. . . . Uphold me according to your promise, that I may live, and let me not be put to shame in my hope!

PSALM 119:11, 50, 93, 116 ESV

Psalm 119 is a 176-verse acrostic poem about the Word of God. Its anonymous author used the Hebrew alphabet to divide it into sections; then he began each verse (or stanza) in that section with that letter. And every verse makes mention of the Word: the law of the Lord, statutes, precepts, testimonies, ways, commandments, righteous judgments, promises, and so on.

Did you see that? Promises. God's promises are found in His Word. And this particular psalmist says several times throughout the psalm that God's promises give life. If you are in doubt, go back through this book. Do any of the promises here deal out death? No. Why not? Because God is all about life! Especially eternal life.

To begin the cycle of life, we must memorize God's Word. Doing so will keep us from sin, which in scripture leads to death. Then we must allow it to grow by meditating on it and obeying it. Even when trials and troubles come, and they will, we have the living Word of God in our hearts to guide us through and bring us out even stronger and more alive. His Word brings life because it is hope. And hope does not make us ashamed or weak, but strong and ready to proclaim the riches of His Word.

> Thy Word is a lamp to my feet,
> A light to my path alway,

To guide and to save me from sin,
And show me the heav'nly way.
Thy Word have I hid in my heart
That I might not sin against thee;
That I might not sin, that I might not sin,
Thy word have I hid in my heart.
Forever, O Lord, is thy Word
Established and fixed on high;
Thy faithfulness unto all men
Abideth forever nigh.

ERNEST O. SELLERS

93. God Seeks to Support His Own

"The eyes of the LORD search the whole earth in order
to strengthen those whose hearts are fully committed to him."
2 CHRONICLES 16:9 NLT

God looks for you. That's right—He seeks you out to bless and
support you in your endeavors. He's your biggest admirer. Before
you came to Christ, He had His eye on you like a sports scout
discovering a star player. After you committed your life to Him,
He forever etched you on His heart and has you on His radar.

The historian who wrote 2 Chronicles used an example
from King Asa's life to illustrate this principle. Asa, a "good"
king in God's sight, took silver and gold from the treasuries
of the temple and his own to pay Ben-hadad, king of Aram in
Damascus, to protect Judah from being invaded by Israel. So
God sent Hanani, one of His prophets, to tell Asa that because
he trusted Aram to save him instead of God Himself, Ben-hadad
would not keep his treaty with Judah.

Hanani spoke these words in 2 Chronicles 16:9 to remind
Asa that nothing is hidden from God; in fact, the Word says
that everything and everyone is laid bare before the eyes of the
Lord (Hebrews 4:13). What we do in secret is no secret to God,
whether it be for good or for evil.

Perhaps you worked hard to make an event a success,
but someone else received recognition. You deserved praise
but received none. Take heart. God saw every good deed you
performed, and no task went unnoticed by Him. He will bless
you for remaining quiet while everyone else was lauded for their
hard work and achievements.

God is omnipresent and omnipotent. He is with us in our
darkest moments as well as the shining ones. He grieves with us

in our sorrow and rejoices in our successes. He not only is with us but is in us. What's more, He is *for* us. God's eyes are on you to bless, not curse you; to help, uphold, encourage, and support you. When you look for God, don't fret—God is already looking out for you.

94. Pray, Seek, and Repent

"If my people who are called by my name will humble themselves and pray and seek my face and turn from their wicked ways, I will hear from heaven and will forgive their sins and restore their land."
2 CHRONICLES 7:14 NLT

This hallmark verse is a call to national prayer and repentance. No acts of Congress or presidential executive order can bring healing to a nation like a prayer breathed from a repentant heart.

God spoke to King Solomon in response to the king's dedicatory prayer of the temple in Jerusalem. "I have heard your prayer and have chosen this place for Myself as a house of sacrifice" (2 Chronicles 7:12 NASB). Then God provided clear instructions for how His people were to respond if they fell away from worshipping God.

First, we must humble ourselves before Him. After all, what is prayer without humility? How can we approach a holy God without surrendering our wills and acknowledging our human frailties? Next, we must earnestly seek God's will and ways. As we wholeheartedly seek God for our country and for our individual lives, He will avail Himself to us. But we must persist in prayer, even after the flesh signals defeat. Finally, and most importantly, we must repent of our sins. What good is seeking God without turning from the very acts of unrighteousness that separate us from Him?

When Solomon prayed, God answered him by night. A cloud, signifying God's power and presence, filled the temple and God promised to cause the pestilence to cease and the much-needed rains to come. King Solomon sought God on behalf of his nation, and God blessed the Israelites.

Every Christian can claim this verse as his or her battle

cry. God has always had a people—the children of Israel and His church today—and He calls on us to pray, seek, and repent. When we do, He promises to hear, forgive, and heal our land.

95. Seek and Find Answers

"Call to Me and I will answer you,
and I will tell you great and mighty things,
which you do not know."
JEREMIAH 33:3 NASB

When you ask someone for a favor, what do you expect to get in return? When you ask someone, presumably a good friend or family member, for food to feed guests, do you expect to receive limp, nearly rotten fruit and vegetables? Of course not!

God's answers are even better. In fact, He always wants to delight us by giving us more than we expect or asked for or even imagined (Ephesians 3:20). His promise to Jeremiah and the people of Judah (who refused to listen to Him or Jeremiah) was that if they called on Him, He would hear and show them "great and mighty things" they hadn't known before.

One aspect of God's Word that the writer of Hebrews brings out is that it is alive. It is a living, breathing entity because it comes out of the mouth of the God of all life. This "aliveness" means that as we grow and mature, God's Word has deeper meaning every time we read it.

Have you ever read a passage of scripture that is familiar to you? Maybe you've even memorized it. Maybe you're tempted to skip over it to something not so familiar. But the Holy Spirit nudges you to read it again, carefully, slowly, and all of a sudden it comes alive with new meaning, a deeper application, a different aspect to consider and meditate on. That's what Jeremiah and the writer of Hebrews meant when they wrote about getting God's perspective on life.

Several times in the psalms, the psalmists speak of calling on the Lord and the benefits of doing so.

"I call upon the LORD, *who is worthy
to be praised, and I am saved from
my enemies." (Psalm 18:3* NASB)
"I will call on God, and the LORD *will
rescue me." (Psalm 55:16* NLT)
*"I will lift up the cup of salvation and
praise the* LORD'S *name for saving
me. . . . I will offer you a sacrifice of
thanksgiving and call on the name
of the* LORD." *(Psalm 116:13, 17* NLT)

God still has so much to show us. Consider asking Him to
do so the next time you sit down to read His Word.

96. Priorities

"Seek the Kingdom of God above all else, and live righteously, and he will give you everything you need."
MATTHEW 6:33 NLT

Jesus had a lot to say about worry and anxiety during His earthly ministry, just as He did before He came to earth and after He ascended into heaven at the end of His time on earth. Why is that? Maybe, just maybe, His people have "trust issues," in today's terminology. (Ya think?)

One of the more well-known passages of scripture is found in the middle of the Sermon on the Mount (Matthew 6:25–34). Jesus reveals that He reads our thoughts and probably knows them better than we do ourselves. He certainly knows the root causes of our worry and anxiety.

The latest statistics say that 95 percent of everything we worry about never comes to anything. In other words, our worrying adds up to a lot of wasted time! Partly because we worry about things over which we have no control.

For example, we can't change our height, but we worry about it. We worry what other people will think about it. (What does it matter?) So we go about slouching (if we're tall) and standing on tiptoes (if we're short). Or we worry about where our next meal is coming from or if we have enough clothes.

Then there are the bigger-ticket items. Our dishwasher breaks. The washer goes berserk. The air conditioner breaks in the middle of a heat wave. Or the car, our only means of transportation, quits running. And there's no money to pay for repairs or replacements.

Jesus tells us that our Father in heaven already knows we have need of these things. So spend time seeking Him, His ways,

His Word, and the end result is that He will provide everything we need to follow Him wholeheartedly.

As the old children's chorus says, "Jesus and others and you." Put seeking the Lord first and everything else will fall into place. . .without the worry and fuss.

97. A Promise to Those Who Wait on Him

But they who wait for the LORD shall renew their strength;
they shall mount up with wings like eagles;
they shall run and not be weary, they shall walk and not faint.
ISAIAH 40:31 ESV

It's hard to conceive of never being tired. In these human bodies it simply isn't possible. Life zaps strength, and no one is immune to weariness. "Even youths shall faint and be weary, and young men shall fall exhausted" (Isaiah 40:30 ESV). No matter how strong we are, life *will* wear us out.

But God is not a mere man. In fact, "The LORD is the everlasting God, the Creator of the ends of the earth. He does not faint or grow weary" (40:28 ESV). He never falls asleep or needs to slumber. There is never a time He is too tired to listen to us or hear our needs. There is never a time He is too weak to defend us or too weary to care for His creation. God is always alert. Full of energy. Strong!

This God of unending strength and energy loves to share His strength with us. "He gives power to the faint, and to him who has no might he increases strength" (40:29 ESV). King David said, "Awesome is God from his sanctuary; the God of Israel—he is the one who gives power and strength to his people" (Psalm 68:35 ESV).

Isaiah told us how to access this strength we need. He said it comes when we wait upon the Lord.

Did you notice there is no admonition to gut it out when we are weary or to force ourselves forward by inner reserves? No, Isaiah simply tells us to *wait*.

Waiting on the Lord reminds us that we are not sufficient on our own. We acknowledge that while our resources are limited,

His are not. In fact, the apostle Paul said he was actually stronger in weakness because that was when he relied most on God's resources.

The strength promised in Isaiah 41 is beyond human ability. It's the strength of an eagle that flies above life's storms, of a runner who doesn't get tired, of one who can walk without ever growing faint.

When we commit ourselves to God's keeping, waiting upon Him for the strength we need, He will not fail us.

98. All Things Are Possible

I can do all things [which He has called me to do] through Him
who strengthens and empowers me [to fulfill His purpose—
I am self-sufficient in Christ's sufficiency; I am ready for
anything and equal to anything through Him who infuses
me with inner strength and confident peace].
PHILIPPIANS 4:13 AMP

The book of Philippians was written when Paul was in prison
in Rome for preaching the Gospel of Jesus Christ. It's the most
positive of all the letters Paul wrote. And some of it is a thank-
you for the gift the church at Philippi had put together for him
to help him in his need.

For prisoners to be fed and kept by taxpayers' money is a
relatively recent development. Definitely in Paul's time, prisoners
had to rely on the help of family and friends for food and clothes
and other needs while they were imprisoned. So a gift from one
of the churches meant a lot to Paul.

He knew they didn't have much, and in chapter 4, Paul told
them while he was grateful for their gift, he didn't really need it, for
he had learned to be content no matter what his circumstances.

Being content in any situation isn't an easy lesson to learn.
And the Lord had allowed many different situations in Paul's life
to teach him this valuable lesson. Have you ever wondered how
he did it?

Verse 13 tells us. He could do anything the Lord asked him
to do through Jesus Christ, who empowered him to do all God
had purposed for Paul to do with his life. The phrase "I am self-
sufficient in Christ's sufficiency" tells us that no matter what
his circumstances, he could be content because Christ was there
with him.

Because Christ was his constant companion, he was "ready for anything and equal to anything through Him who infuse[d him] with inner strength and confident peace."

Jesus Christ through the Holy Spirit is ready to do the same for you. Contentment, peace, and even joy are possible when we allow Him to empower us to fulfill His purposes through us.

99. God Gives Us Words

"So make up your minds not to prepare beforehand to defend yourselves; for I will give you utterance and wisdom which none of your opponents will be able to resist or refute."

LUKE 21:14–15 NASB

Some people seem to have an answer for everything. Do you know anyone like that? Maybe you are one. But that isn't the reality for most of us.

Did you know that public speaking is the number one fear people admit to? That would include getting up and giving a testimony or being on the witness stand in court. For some even standing in front of a classroom of peers strikes terror to their heart—their mind goes blank, and a one-minute speech feels like an eternity!

Paul told Timothy in the second letter he wrote to him that no one came to stand with him when he had his first hearing before a court of law. Maybe they were afraid they would be arrested, too, or that they would become tongue-tied and not be able to speak for Paul. Whatever the reason, Paul went on to tell Timothy that the Lord stood with him and gave him the words to speak boldly for the cause of Christ (2 Timothy 4:16–17).

Jesus told His disciples not to prepare fancy speeches ahead of time when they were arrested for preaching the Gospel and would have to defend themselves in a court of law. He promised He would give them (and us when we are in the same position) the words to say when they were needed. And what words they will be! Words so full of wisdom none of our opponents will be able to say anything in response.

The day is fast approaching when we may have to rely on this promise that we don't need to prepare ahead of time what we are to say. We can take comfort in knowing He will give us the words to say when the time does come. We can finally put that fear of public speaking behind us.

100. God Gives Us Wisdom

If any of you lacks wisdom [to guide him through a decision
or circumstance], he is to ask of [our benevolent] God,
who gives to everyone generously and without rebuke
or blame, and it will be given to him.
JAMES 1:5 AMP

Many years ago, in a high school honors literature class, the
teacher gave an opportunity for students to invite their "religious"
leaders to come to the public school's classroom to present their
beliefs. The teacher wished to use the students' recent reading and
discussion of philosophy in "testing" these leaders as to why they
believed the way they did.

A Catholic priest, a Baptist minister, a rabbi, and Mormon
elders accepted the invitation to speak. Several of the students
were believers, and they were quick to understand that the
Mormon elders who spoke took James 1:5 out of context to
justify Joseph Smith's writing the Book of Mormon. The elders
told the class that Joseph was confused by what the "traditional"
church taught, and so he asked God to show him the truth.
And that's when he received his first vision that led later to the
teachings of the Mormon church.

Since that was the only scripture the elders used and all the
rest of their presentation was from the Book of Mormon, most
of the class members rejected their presentation as faulty, even
those who didn't profess to believe the Bible.

One of the first tenets of true biblical scholarship is that
scripture interprets scripture. We must teach scripture in context.
James wrote this letter, placing this verse at the end of a passage
that tells us how to respond when we find ourselves in adverse
circumstances—with pure joy.

Joy is a totally counterintuitive response to hard situations, but we do have a resource, a constant Companion, who understands. Nothing ever surprises Him. Nothing ever takes Him off guard. After all, He is sovereign over all things. He controls everything. And Satan can do nothing without His permission (Job 1–2).

So the next time you are faced with a situation to which you don't know how to react or respond, ask God. He never fails to fulfill His promises.